11.99

Always a Wedding

Beginning, Renewing and Rescuing Marriage

By
Dr. James Lee Collins

THE BOOK HOUSE
Over 100, 000 books instock!
480 Veterans Memorial Hwy SW
Mableton, GA 30126
770-944-3275

To Sandra, my Wife

When I first met you in 1966, your beautiful features of personality,
appearance, intelligence and Christian fidelity were impressive.
However, your quality of being authentic won my heart.
You were free to be genuinely yourself.
This is the one attribute that sustains love and marriage for the entire
journey. It has been so for us.
One of the driving motivations behind writing this
book is for the purpose of
dedicating it to you
and saying
"Thank You for giving me
Your Love That Completes My Life."

Table of Contents

ACKNOWLEDGMENTS

E ach of us is a beneficiary of others. Although we are unique with qualities and features no other person has, our essential nature reflects the influences and contributions through the days and years of our lives of family, friends, strangers, teachers, leaders, and children. I am a living witness of this.

Also, this book is not something I have produced alone. It is an accumulation of innumerable experiences, informative lessons, and insightful stories from many people. I, therefore, want to acknowledge the generous blessings God has brought to me though the diversity of people who have intersected my life, especially at the Peachtree Christian Church in Atlanta, Georgia.

The wedding ministry began there in 1925, when the sanctuary was dedicated as a Cathedral for Atlanta where any bride and groom wanting a beautiful place for a Christian wedding would be welcomed. When I became the Senior Pastor there in 1986, we expanded this signature ministry with a Wedding Guild of more than forty people for whom I will forever be grateful. They provided free services at rehearsals and wedding ceremonies to assist the bridal party and the officiating minister in achieving an orderly, inspiring, and memorable experience as a new home was being established.

In particular, I want to thank my insightful and wonderful wife Sandra. We have been best friends and partners for forty three years in the pursuit of marriage. We have learned so much together, and from our daughters, Leslie and LeAnne, born on the same day, June 27, four years apart. They have journeyed with us enduring all the demands of Christian ministry and receiving the marvelous benefits of unconditional love. I am so very grateful to them for encouraging me with their patience and helpfulness.

My sincere appreciation is given to Dr. Bonnie Harvey and Dr. Brad Miller for giving editorial guidance, and to Dr. Patricia Rife who provided Senior Editorial direction in key passages and formatting of this book. I want to commend my special friend, Barbara Youngleson, who designed the cover for "Always A Wedding." I am also grateful to my sister, Mary Helen Williams, and dear friends, Dianne Watson, Sandy Smith, and Ruth Ann Tyler, for reading my manuscript. They proved that some of my English teachers taught me in vain, but now make me look scholarly with all the grammatical and punctuation corrections they contributed to this endeavor.

Finally, I want to express gratitude to each couple who reads and benefits from this book, to each Church, community, organization, and learning institution that encourages its reading, and to individuals who present this book as a gift to a couple BEGINNING their marriage, RENEWING their marriage, or RESCUING their marriage.

To God be the Glory,
Dr. Jim Collins

FOREWARD

"I have told everyone I know that if the <u>Wall Street Journal</u> did a front page article on the profile of a genuine authentic pastor in America, it would profile Dr. Jim Collins and have his picture smiling with approval upon all couples who value marriage.

His warm, caring and authentic personality endeared him to my entire family when my daughter was married at his Church in Atlanta, Georgia. This book is a must read for everyone who still believes a pastor is a shepherd!" Dr. Kirk Nowery

Dr. Kirk Nowery was the Chaplain for 12 years of the
Miami Dolphins Football Team.
As the former Pastor of one of America's largest congregations based in
Miami, Florida, Rev. Nowery served as President of INJOY Stewardship
Services, Ministry Leader of Hope Partners and
Samaritan's Purse of the Billy Graham Evangelistic Association.

INTRODUCTION

Always a Wedding! In fact, human life began with a wedding: read Genesis Chapters 1 and 2 in the Bible. Every human culture and civilization throughout time had weddings. But why is there "always" a wedding?

Love gives us the answer. In the New Testament I John 4:16b declares, "God is Love, and those who abide in Love abide in God, and God abides in them." The God of Love who created man and woman in His image designed them in Love, by Love, and for Love. Our greatest need and desire is to love and be loved. First Corinthians 13:13 affirms this to be true. The Apostle Paul states, "Three things abide; faith, hope, and love, these three; and the greatest of these is love."

Since God is love, everyone created in the Image of God naturally seeks love. Our souls are restless until we are one with our Creator through faith. When there is oneness with God we experience love. Hence, the essence of our human nature is love. A man, therefore, seeks completion in the shared love with a woman. A woman yearns for wholeness through the giving and receiving of love with a man. During the period of creation, the only time God said something was not good was after man was given life. God then said, "It is not good for man to be alone." So God created woman from man's side to be a partner with him. She was not created from the head to be superior or from the feet to be inferior. She was given life from the side of man nearest his heart to be equal in worth, value, purpose, meaning, and fulfillment.

In this book, certain Biblical principles are identified that can guide couples into a "forever" covenant of love and faithfulness. There is no greater return a couple can receive for their investment of loving, honoring, and cherishing each other as long as life lasts than the shared journey of happiness with one's best friend.

When I asked Sandra in 1967 to be my wife, I was yearning for completion. I wanted to give her my love and faithfulness for as long as I lived. I also sought her love and companionship with all my heart. I then asked her an unrehearsed question, "What do you want from a husband?" Without any hesitation or forethought, she said, "I want my husband to love me." It was surprising and satisfying to realize we each were seeking fulfillment that only love could provide. Our response was natural — for we were designed by the God of Love to love and be loved! Hearts are restless and constantly searching until true love is received and given. When we exchanged rings on our wedding day the letters "Y.L.C.M.L." were engraved within each of them. They represent what we found in each other to be true: "YOUR LOVE COMPLETES MY LIFE."

In this book "Always A Wedding", many of the marvelous things we have learned about love and marriage, anger and patience, failure and success are discussed. The twenty one chapters are based on the twenty one different sermons I gave as Senior Pastor during the "Wedding Bells Service" at the Peachtree Christian Church in Atlanta, Georgia. On the second Sunday of every January, married couples are invited during the worship service to renew their vows of marriage. It is not only a way to experience a new beginning as a New Year starts. It is also a time to reclaim the sacred meaning of marriage.

As long as human life exists man and woman will search for love. When love is realized, the commitment to give and receive love inevitably follows. One confirmation of this comes from motion picture sound engineers. Some years ago they listed the most dramatic sounds that moved the emotions of people in their industry. These sounds included: a baby's cry, the blast of a siren, screeching automobile tires, the roar of a forest fire, a fog horn from a ship at sea, the slow drip of water, galloping horses, a distant train whistle, the howl of a dog, and the music of a wedding march. These sound experts determined that one sound above all others creates more charisma, arouses more expectancy, makes a person's pulse go faster, and brings more tears. This superlative sound is the wedding march! They claim it reaches the deepest yearnings of the human heart more than any other.

Hence, there will "Always Be A Wedding."

CHAPTER ONE

GOD'S FIRST GIFT

Genesis 1: 26a-28a, *"Then God said, 'Let us make humankind in our image, according to our likeness; and let them have dominion... 'So God created humankind in his image, in the image of God he created them; male and female he created them. God blessed them, and God said to them, 'Be fruitful and multiply...'. And it was so. God saw everything that he had made, and indeed, it was very good."*

An English college Professor wrote on the chalkboard, "A woman without her man is nothing." He then asked his students to punctuate the sentence. All the men in the class wrote: "A woman, without her man, is nothing." All the women in the class wrote: "A woman: without her, man is nothing."

The Professor reported the results to the class and said, "Each of the two ways of punctuating this sentence is correct. God created man and woman wonderfully different in so many ways. Yet, God created them equal in value and purpose. In His image, He created them male and female. Man fulfills woman and woman completes man."

This is God's plan for human life. Man and woman were created in God's image. The first gift they received from God was marriage. God joined man and woman together, and they became one. Before God established a government, or any other entity or institution, God created marriage. Jesus affirmed this as God's first great gift to humanity when he said in Mark 10:6-9. "From the beginning of creation, 'God made them male and female. For this reason, a man shall leave his father and mother and be joined to his wife, and the two shall become one flesh.' So they are no longer two, but one flesh. Therefore what God has joined together, let no one separate."

Just consider this "first" gift God chose to present to man and woman. God could have designed eternal wealth for them to enjoy, a nation for them to rule, powers that could move the stars in the heavens. But God valued one gift above all others. Marriage was the perfect one that could bring happiness and fulfillment to man and woman as no other gift could.

During my pastoral ministry in Brunswick, Georgia in the mid 1960s, I learned something very special about a gift. I was not married and lived in a parsonage next door to the First Christian Church. The Catholic Church was two blocks away, and the Rectory where the four priests lived was just around the corner. The priests and I became good friends. We participated together in several community ministries. The priests and I had in common the fact that each of us was not married. They had an advantage over me, however. They had a "house mother" who cooked their food, cleaned their Rectory, and laundered their clothes. They finally admitted my inferior situation in comparison to theirs. Being moved with compassion the priests gave me an open invitation to come to their table for evening meals. I frequently accepted their offer. I not only enjoyed delicious food. I also benefitted from active theological discussions, and aggressive debates about the differences between the Roman Catholic and Protestant teachings of scripture.

After Sandra and I married in 1967, it was clear to me that my position had dramatically changed from inferior to superior compared to that of my Catholic priest brothers. They did not take offense however. We remained friends although their dinner table was no longer an option for me.

Soon after we married, an opportunity opened for us to go to Atlanta where I could benefit from an advanced course in Clinical Pastoral Education. When we announced our plans to leave Brunswick, the Catholic priests invited us to a dinner at the Yacht Club on St. Simons Island, Georgia. We gladly accepted their gracious invitation. Following a wonderful meal and delightful conversations about the table, the Senior Priest, Father Collins, stood to speak.

He began with humorous recollections of my bachelorhood days. He told of the free meals served to me at their Rectory. He explained that as a result of my hearty eating, he had to give an account for the extra expense to their budget. He simply noted in the ledger that these were meals "provided to the needy." Then he began to explain the nature of a gift. Because he was committed to the Vow of Poverty as a Roman

Catholic Priest, things in general did not mean much to him. He confessed that some earthly possessions however, had become very important to him. Giving any of them up would be very difficult for him. But he had learned that expressing heartfelt love for someone was best done with a very important gift. The most valuable gifts are those that belong to you, and represent a strong emotional attachment. They are the ones hard to give up. But love makes it easy and rewarding for the giver.

Father Collins went on to say, "As we were preparing to say farewell to our friends, Jim and Sandra, with this dinner tonight, I wanted to give them a gift. The one possession that meant so much to me over the years was the brass and marble candle holders that I brought as a young priest to America from Ireland. They have been on the mantle of our Rectory for some time. I now want to give these tokens of love and appreciation to our friends. Jim and Sandra, I give these to you for your new home in Atlanta on behalf of the other priests because they mean so much to me."

This Catholic priest defined for me the nature of a true gift. It is one of your most valued possessions that only love could move you to give to another person. As we try to contemplate God's First Gift to man and woman, I believe we have to recognize that it was the One gift that meant the most to God: the Gift of Marriage. The true Image of God is Love. In the New Testament, I John 4:16 declares, "God is love, and those who abide in love abide in God, and God abides in them." Love reflects God's very Image in every human.

This was affirmed by the Apostle Paul in what is called "The Love Chapter of The Holy Bible": I Corinthians 13. In verse 13 there are three great gifts that abide, "Faith, Hope, and Love, these three. But the greatest of these is Love." I John 4:19, makes it clear that, "We love because God first loved us." While in Jerusalem one day a Jewish lawyer asked Jesus, "Teacher, which commandment in the law is the greatest." Jesus answered in Matthew 22:37-39, "You shall love the Lord your God with all your heart, and with all your soul, and with all your mind. This is the greatest and first commandment. And a second is like it: You shall love your neighbor as yourself."

God — who is the Alpha and the Omega, the Beginning and the End — is Perfect and Holy in every way. His most valuable gift is Love. In giving His best to the first man and woman, God gave them His Very Image, Love, which makes true marriage possible. Marriage is the means of giving and receiving God's Love in the most complete fulfilling way a man and woman can know. God is neither male nor female. Yet, God created us man and woman, and designed our bodies to be joined together as one. When man and woman are united in marriage with the bonds of love and faithfulness, the very Image of God is realized.

Marriage is a personal-sexual-spiritual-emotional partnership ordained and instituted by God. Through this Divine Gift, husband and wife are to share in the creation of life with God by giving birth to children. Genesis 1:28 decrees God's assignment for marriage: "God blessed them, and God said to them, 'Be fruitful and multiply...'"

Since God alone established marriage, He owns the "Patent for Marriage." A patent is the legal authorization of ownership. A patent safeguards the exclusive property, domain, and use of what has been created by another. Although God doesn't need any legal safeguards for what is His, it is reassuring to know that human institutions maintain the legal rights of an inventor by awarding a patent which designates ownership. Therefore, God owns marriage. It is one of His most valued possessions. God lovingly gives it to a man and woman who commit themselves to the **covenant** of faithfulness, and are willing to live for each other's <u>highest</u> good.

Yet we are reminded daily of the pain and turmoil that marital failure causes. We live in a fallen world. We know that each of us can be driven by selfish desires and actions. In a given moment, each of us can violate the vow we made to "Love, Honor, and Cherish" the one we married. It is not easy to maintain marriage as God intended it to be. Even though God's Gift of Marriage is pure and filled with the potential of happiness for a husband and wife, our human nature makes it very difficult to experience the ideal of God's purpose. Our many flaws and failures cloud the Image of God in our partnership of marriage. God's Image of Love too often is replaced with images of anger, impatience, disappointment, and failure to be true to all that we promised. Yet, God's intentions for marriage will forever represent His first Gift to the ones created in His Image. Love will always be the Greatest Gift in the world no matter how many times we fail to give and receive it.

Some years ago Sandra and I had the privilege of going to New York the week before Christmas. The highlight of our trip was going to the Broadway Play *"Les Miserables."* While sitting in the second row of that theater, I was surprised that some words coming from the stage reached out and embraced me. They have never let me go. The words were, "To love another person is to <u>see</u> the face of God."

It is true! We see the very Image of God when a husband and wife give and receive love with unselfish delight in their marriage.

CHAPTER TWO

PARTNERS SIDE BY SIDE

Genesis 2: 18-25, *"Then the Lord God said, 'It is not good that the man should be alone; I will make him a helper as his partner...' So the Lord God caused a deep sleep to fall upon the man, and he slept; then He took one of his ribs and closed up its place with flesh. And the rib that the Lord God had taken from the man He made into a woman and brought her to the man. Then the man said, 'This at last is bone of my bones and flesh of my flesh; this one shall be called Woman, for out of Man this one was taken.' Therefore a man leaves his father and his mother and clings to his wife, and they become one flesh. And the man and his wife were both naked and were not ashamed."*

A distinguished couple in their early forties stopped at a service station to refuel their luxury sedan. It had been a long drive, and they both got out of the car to stretch their legs. The service attendant was startled when he thought he recognized the woman. He enthusiastically asked, "Connie, is that you?" She turned and remembered him as her high school boyfriend. They joined hands and laughed with fond memories. She then introduced her husband, Bob, who was shocked to see this display of affection. As they were driving back onto the highway, he asked, "Just who was that guy that you were so glad to see?"

Connie explained that he was her first real boyfriend from high school. She confessed that he was more serious about the relationship than she was. Bob then sarcastically said, "It's a good thing you didn't marry him. You would have been stuck with a greasy car mechanic." She was not amused. She then said, "If I had married him, he would have become President of the bank instead of you."

There is some truth in Connie's claim. It has been observed for centuries that behind every successful man there is a good woman! After creating man, God knew that something was missing. God said, "It is not good for man to be alone. I will make him a helper as his partner." In order to bring completion, God created woman. Man fulfills woman and woman fulfills man.

Woman was created from man's side to represent equality. She was created not from the head to suggest superiority, nor from the foot to indicate a subservient role. Her life came from the side of man nearest his heart. A partnership was born for man and woman to walk side by side. God's blueprint for a fulfilling marriage was presented for all couples to follow. God gave Himself for a personal relationship with man and woman, and the covenant of marriage as the sacred relationship that brings completion to man and woman. It is still surprising to Sandra and me that we intuitively had the letters "YLCML" inscribed inside our wedding rings, reminding us that "Your Love Completes My Life." We were not speaking theologically or trying to be Biblical. We were just expressing what our hearts were experiencing. The love and partnership we were sharing were a marvelous discovery of becoming complete as man and woman, as husband and wife.

It was later in our marriage that we realized that our experience was the natural intention of God according to His blueprint for marriage. Genesis 1:27 tells us that "God created man in His own image, in the image of God He created man; male and female He created them." Although they were created with equal status and value in God's image, they were made distinct with different roles that are complimentary. Man was created first to give spiritual leadership and protection for marriage. Woman was created to complete man for God said in Genesis 2:18, "It was not good for man to be alone. I will make him a helper as his partner." In order to be fruitful and multiply as God's blueprint designates, man could not do this without a partner. God created woman as man's helper to complement him in performing the task of having dominion over the earth and being fruitful by bearing children.

The word "helper" in Hebrew is *"ezer kenegdo."* It means a helper who is a perfect fit. It is a great compliment to woman to be named "helper". In the vast majority of cases when the word "ezer" is used in the Old Testament, it is a reference to God. Exodus 18:4 says, "The God of my father was my help, and delivered me from the sword of Pharaoh."

Psalm 20:2, refers to God as help from the sanctuary as Psalm 33:20 declares, "We wait in hope for the Lord; He is our help and our shield." On a board above the deck of our mountain home In Young Harris, Georgia are written the words from Psalm 121, "I lift up my eyes unto the hills...my help comes from the Lord." Therefore, God created Adam and Eve in His image, and gave Eve the quality of His own nature which is to be "helper." In no way does this mean inferior or subordinate. It is the expression of true love. God loved Israel and was helper to His people. A wife loves her husband and seeks to be his helper.

After more than 43 years of marriage, I can honestly say that Sandra has been my helper. There are many other attributes of Sandra's life that have enriched our partnership. But the first and most valuable one that I can name which has enabled me to become the man, husband, father, and Christian Pastor that I am is "helper." Although we have had our differences and disagreements, she has always been my cheerleader. She has encouraged me to learn and grow, to dream and set goals, to attempt tasks that seemed impossible to achieve, and to stand by my side in all our endeavors for God, family, Church, and community. As my wife, she continues to be my helper.

This was God's plan for marriage from the very beginning. Therefore, in receiving woman as his helper and partner, Adam exclaimed, "This is now bone of my bones, and flesh of my flesh", Genesis 2:23. Adam called her woman, and he named her Eve. In Hebrew, man is "*ish*," and woman is "*ishshah*." The word *Ishshah* shows compatibility and linkage to man in the relationship of marriage. But there is a difference between "*ish*" and "*ishshah*." Ishshah means "soft." She was taken from man's side. Man is "*ish*," which suggests strength and roughness to work hard. Woman is also strong (*ish*), but soft (*shah*). Together they form a perfect union to compliment and fulfill each other.

In creating us as man and woman, God changed what was not good (man being alone) to a relationship that was "very good" as stated in Genesis 1:31. We now can read the pronouncement of God's first gift to humanity as it is beautifully stated in Genesis 2:24, "Therefore, a man leaves his father and his mother and clings to his wife, and they become one flesh." Jesus our Lord and Savior quoted this as an affirmation of God's plan for marriage in Mark 10:7-9, and stated, "Therefore, what God has joined together, let no one separate."

As I reflect on our relationship in marriage, I have endeavored to provide Sandra with love and encouragement for her to fulfill her potential in every way possible. She has given me love and respect through our years together as my "helper" enabling me to be my best self. The two words that best describe our partnership are "Best Friends." We have many friends and wonderful family members. But there is no question in our minds and hearts as to who is our best friend. We are to each other the best friend we have.

Some years ago I was counseling with a couple to be married in the awesome beauty of our Gothic Sanctuary at the Peachtree Christian Church in Atlanta. The bride asked me a question. She wanted to know if it would be alright for her to come down the center aisle to begin her wedding with her little Pekingese dog in her arms. I was shocked to hear this unusual request. I diplomatically explained that we had various policies for a wedding ceremony designed to maintain the reverence and dignity of our place of worship. But realizing she wasn't impressed with my response, I asked her why she wanted to do this. She adamantly stated, "My dog, 'Precious,' is my best friend." I smiled and said, "Really!" I then looked at her fiancée and asked, "Well, who is he?" Somewhat apologetically she said, "I guess I never thought of him as my best friend." After the dogless wedding she told me that the best part of their premarital counseling was discovering who her best friend really was.

When a man and woman commit themselves to each other and to God in the Covenant of Marriage, I believe one of the main focuses of their lives together should be "friendship." Friendship is the glue that holds a couple together as they negotiate responsibilities, meals, entertainment, hobbies, schedules, financial matters, and raising children. In all these shared issues and decisions of married life, growing as best friends is the greatest joy of being husband and wife. God intends for your partner to be the most intimate person in your life. It is natural and right for this person to be your best friend.

Some of the qualities of a best friend that can guide a couple into a successful marriage are the following seven that I have found true in our marriage.

THE FIRST IS AUTHENTICITY. It is essential that a best friend be genuine. The motto of my high school was, "To <u>Be</u> Rather Than To Seem." This was a guiding principle for me to become a real person. It was also one that caused me to determine the character of other people. This was the predominate quality of the young woman I met on St. Simons Island, Georgia in 1966. She became my wife the following year. I have admired her authenticity through the years more than any other aspect of her life. Almost everything else in life changes such as our appearance, status, and possessions. But the one quality that is most valued is being a genuine person without pretense. Sandra won my love and devotion with her authenticity more than any other feature. I have endeavored to provide her with this same quality. It continues to be the basis of our friendship.

THE SECOND IS ACCEPTANCE. A best friend accepts you as you are with the clear understanding that you are not perfect and never will be. Yet, there is mutual permission to be who you are with the feelings, values, and beliefs that are yours. Listening to each other is satisfying because you feel accepted even when there are disagreements. You delight in each other's presence. There is no one you had rather be with than your best friend. Sandra often tells me that she enjoys working in the yard with me, or accomplishing a project together. Perhaps it is her way of getting me to do what is needed around the house. But even so, I delight in her presence. I enjoy being with her and doing things together. We accept each other unconditionally.

THE THIRD IS AFFIRMATION. We all need affirmation for who we are and for what we do that is important. Our best friend is the first to provide this gift. The one who knows us best has the power to lift us to our highest level of achievement. Their affirmation gives us confidence to believe in ourselves, and to pursue worthwhile tasks that need to be accomplished. Sandra, my best friend from the very beginning of our marriage, has been my cheerleader. She listened more attentively to my sermons than anyone. Most of the time she gave me an approving smile from the second pew in front of the pulpit as I concluded each sermon. I could almost hear her say, "Well done, Jim. That was very meaningful." Through the years when a couple was inquiring about my performing their wedding Sandra would always say, "He is the best!" Whether or not others agreed with her biased opinion, it didn't matter to me. The one who knew me best always gave me the affirmation that motivated me to do my best. In every way I could I contributed to her self confidence, and encouraged her to invest her many talents in the activities of her life. One of my greatest accomplishments was getting Sandra to "horse trade" during her shopping by negotiating for a price less than the asking one. She now is very good at this skill, especially when we travel to other countries. Each time she stands up for herself in ways like this, I say with a big grin, "Way to go, Sandra!" As best friends we increase each other's self-esteem.

THE FOURTH IS ACCOUNTABILITY. A best friend is trustworthy and honest. A promise given is a promise kept if at all possible. There are no real secrets between best friends. Their lives are transparent. They are committed to the truth. Even if telling the truth means you are going to be in trouble, a best friend is accountable to being honest no matter what. It also assures the other that you will maintain confidentiality. Personal matters are not shared with family, associates, neighbors, or other friends without permission from your best friend. When a mistake occurs or a problem develops, you don't play "the blame game". You are accountable for your actions to your best friend.

THE FIFTH IS AMIABILITY. To be "amiable" means you seek to have a good, friendly and positive nature. You avoid criticism and a negative disposition whenever possible. You are friendly and pro-active. You are fun loving and playful. You value a good sense of humor, and enjoy a hearty laugh. My Dad and Mom were married for fifty-seven years. She often said, "One of the best things about our marriage was he made me laugh every day." Being amiable also means you are more eager to see the good in others than the bad. Scripture teaches us in Philippians 4:8-9, "Whatever is true, whatever is honorable, whatever is just, whatever is pure, whatever is pleasing, whatever is commendable, if there is any excellence and if there is anything worthy of praise, think about these things." This quality alone nurtures a best friend relationship for a life time. You delight is being together when each is amiable.

THE SIXTH IS APPRECIATION. In the movie, "Fiddler On The Roof," Tevye asks his wife, "Do you love me?" She is not amused. She reminds him of her twenty five years of devotion, washing his clothes, preparing his meals, raising their children, and sleeping in his bed. "Why.." she asks him, "do you want to know if I love you?" Yet he was really asking, "Do you appreciate me?" Many others in our daily lives may never express appreciation for who we are and what we do — but our best friend always does! The grateful words, the thoughtful notes, the special gifts, the compliments spoken to family and friends are predictable expressions of appreciation from a best friend. We need appreciation to give assurance of being loved: being appreciative is to "count our blessings". A husband and wife find appreciation more valuable than silver and gold so far as their marriage is concerned.

THE SEVENTH IS APOLOGY. A best friend is <u>willing</u> to apologize when a wrong is done. Realizing the value of a best friend relationship and the damage an inconsiderate act can do, an apology is always necessary. A best friend, even reluctantly, will provide this healing medicine when guilty of hurting the other. This was one of the flaws I brought into our marriage. I had always taken pride in thinking I was right. I was raised a Christian, trained in the Boy Scouts, made good grades in school, and became an ordained minister. It was a surprise for me to learn from my wife that I was not always right in my thinking, decisions, and actions! When confronted with a mistake or inconsiderate act, it was difficult early in our marriage for me to say, "I am sorry." I had a ready defense to justify whatever I did, or failed to do. Sandra taught me the importance of apologizing. After missing several evening meals and getting the cold shoulder, I quickly learned that a best friend admits when he is wrong! I have become a better person because of this lesson.

Equally important is the act of forgiveness. As soon as I honestly confessed my wrong, Sandra would forgive me. I have practiced the art of forgiving her as well. Jesus our Lord taught and demonstrated for us the necessity of forgiving others as we have been forgiven.

God's plan for a successful marriage, therefore, is based on the partnership and "shared seasons of life" for a man and woman, understood most clearly as "Best Friends." The qualities of best friends are:

1) Authenticity
2) Acceptance
3) Affirmation
4) Accountability
5) Amiability
6) Appreciation
7) Apology

CHAPTER THREE

A COVENANT OR A CONTRACT?

Ephesians 5:21-25, *"Be subject to one another out of reverence for Christ. Wives, be subject to your husbands as you are to the Lord...Husbands, love your wives, just as Christ loved the Church and gave Himself up for her."*

Marriage is a commitment. It is a relationship for life that requires the investment of your best effort. However, the commitment to marriage seems to be more demanding than any other promise we make.

For example, a couple had grown in their love for each other during a two year relationship. She was very eager to get married. He was reluctant to make the big commitment. She finally confronted him with this observation. She said, "Help me understand your problem with making a commitment. You have a thirty year mortgage obligation on your new house. You just signed a five year lease on a new car. You have a lifetime membership at the fitness center for $25 dollars a month. Yet, you are not willing to make a commitment to the one you claim to love with all your heart. What is it that I'm not understanding?"

It is often the case in our Western culture for a person to think of marriage as just another commitment or contract. Yet, the responsibility of keeping such a contract can be an uncertain probability. A contract involves two parties whose promises are usually based on a 50/50 agreement. If one fails to live up to his or her promises, the contract has an option clause that permits an exit to their "living together arrangement." Unfortunately exiting is what many couples decide to do when the disappointments of their marriage seem insurmountable.

This contractual marriage is not what God intended. Marriage as God designed it to be is a covenant involving three, and not just a contract involving two. God explains in Ephesians 5:21 that a husband and wife are to be subject to each other out of reverence for Christ. Being subject to, or submitting to each other means a husband and wife are to endeavor to give 100% to their relationship as an expression of their love. The Greek word for "submit" and "love" carries a similar meaning. They both imply giving oneself up to someone, to sacrifice with acts of self-giving for the good of another. No one is perfect, and there will be many days when only 60% or 70% of effort is given in loving devotion to the marriage. But even this will be far greater than the 50/50 terms of the contract of marriage. The goal of a covenant marriage is to always give your very best no matter what.

Clearly, the goal of true marriage should be for a husband and wife every day to give 100% of their devotion, consideration, and thoughtful acts of love to each other. Even when they get angry and frustrated with each other they can and should be loving and respectful. If they seek to live for each other's highest good in these ways, it is possible to enjoy all 200% of their investments! They each put in a 100% effort, and together they benefit from a 200% dividend. The selfish "I" is sacrificed out of love for the interdependent "we." All that the husband is and has are to belong to the wife. All that she is and has are to belong to the husband. They no longer think and live as before marriage on the basis of "me" and "mine". They now live for each other on the basis of "us and ours". When this is realized, life doesn't get any better. Happiness and fulfillment become a reality that satisfies their hearts.

This is what those in the contract of marriage want. But they will never have it because the contract only calls for each to give 50% of themselves to the relationship. Then when failure and divorce come, all the Judge allows each to have is 50% of what they have "invested and accumulated." That is all they brought to the marriage, and that is all they can take away when the contract ends. I recently read the sad language of a judge's "Final Judgment and Decree of Divorce." It said, "It is considered, ordered and decreed by the Court that the marriage contract heretofore entered into between the parties to this case, from and after this date, be and is set aside and dissolved as fully and effectually as if no such contract had ever been made or entered into." A couple who begins the journey of love does not intend or want it to end. God certainly doesn't for His Words are clear in the Old Testament Book of Malachi 2:16, "For I hate divorce." We all do. It doesn't have to be this way if a couple will <u>choose</u>

the Covenant of Marriage instead of the legal contract of living together. Jesus our Lord affirms God's purpose for a couple who seeks to be subject to each other out of reverence for Christ: "So they are no longer two, but one flesh. Therefore what God has joined together, let no one separate" (Mark 10:8-9).

Unfortunately, a marriage will die unless a husband and wife are giving more than 50%. A wife can give 75%, but if the husband only contributes 40%, the marriage will not survive. The husband can give 85%, but the marriage will not live if the wife only gives 45%. The absolute minimum for marriage to live is for the wife and husband to give 51% so there is some overlap of unselfish love. If not, the inevitable will happen. The hopes and dreams of that kind of marriage will result in failure.

However, in the Covenant of Marriage, there are three persons: husband, wife, and Christ. When marriage is limited to only two persons who have the full responsibility of succeeding or failing, the full potential of marriage is never realized. In the Covenant of Marriage where Christ is honored and His help welcomed, a couple's love is fortified each day with His Eternal and unending Love. The success of their marriage doesn't depend on them alone. It also depends upon the Presence of Christ. He is the unfailing source of true success in marriage. He is the strength of a lasting and happy marriage. He is the One who gives to a man and woman the heavenly gifts of Love, Faithfulness, Unselfishness, Patience, Gentleness, Courage, Joy, Peace, Grace, and Forgiveness to share with each other. These sustain marriage through the good and the bad times of life. Therefore, the success of Covenant Marriage doesn't depend just on the best efforts of a husband and wife. It depends upon their daily faithfulness to Jesus Christ who is faithful to generously provide them with the fruit of the Holy Spirit.

One of the best explanations of marriage as contract or covenant that I have heard was given by Chip Ingram at a pastor's conference in Atlanta, Georgia. He was the newly appointed president and CEO of Walk Thru The Bible Ministry in Atlanta. Rev. Ingram reflected "This comparison of the 'two kinds of marriage' is not original with me. " He defined marriage as two obvious <u>choices</u> in our society. One was a prescription of happiness presented by a large segment of the entertainment world through its movies, music, magazines, and books. The other is God's plan as revealed in scripture for happiness, fulfillment, and meaningful living. In his book, "Love, Sex, and Lasting Relationships," Rev. Ingram describes these choices.

The first one offers the following four steps:

1. Find the right person who makes you feel the right way and measures up to your expectations.
2. Fall in love with all the romantic yearnings of enjoying that person for the rest of your life.
3. Fix your hopes and dreams for happiness and fulfillment upon this person.
4. Failure usually occurs, so continue repeating steps one, two, and three.

The second plan also offers four steps to happiness and fulfillment:

1. Seek to become the right person through faith in God and living according to His Word and Will.
2. Walk in love with patience, kindness, forgiveness, and a positive attitude.
3. Fix your hopes and dreams for happiness and fulfillment upon God, who is the source of love.
4. If failure occurs, then repeat steps one, two, and three.

The popularity of the first plan has increased the brokenness of marriage and family life. The New York Times Almanac stated that America had 4.3 million divorced people in 1970. By the 21st century, the number has grown to over 19 million people. The divorce rate in the last few years has declined in part because many couples "live together" without the commitment to marriage. Yet over 41% of first marriages ended in divorce. This is not what anyone wants. Mere "living together" doesn't produce the happiness and fulfillment that a man and woman yearn to have. Plan one, therefore, is obviously not a wise choice for investing your love.

Plan two is far more promising for the success and happiness of marriage. Instead of expecting the one you love to meet your needs and keep you happy twenty four hours a day, you look to God who is the source of lasting love, joy, and peace. Instead of trying to change the one you love into the person of your fantasy, you endeavor to become the unique person of integrity and strength God has designed you to be. In these ways a husband and wife become persons of character with personal values that enrich the lives of those around you. They are able to love, forgive, encourage, and rejoice in the goodness of life which reflects their true nature of having been created in God's very image. They become more attractive to each other, and with positive and optimistic attitudes, they are more fun to live with as best friends.

I can witness to the effectiveness of God's covenant plan of marriage. After 43 years of marriage with Sandra, I can honestly say our partnership is more valuable than any other experience we have had, any achievement we have accomplished, or any property we have accumulated. Next to our salvation in Jesus Christ, we know marriage is God's supreme gift for a man and woman who are willing to live according to God's terms of covenant. In order to receive and maintain this great treasure of life, we have learned that it is worth all the effort, sacrifice, compromise, and patience that the Covenant of Marriage requires. The dividends of this lifelong investment are greater and more joyful than any other this world can offer.

The key that unlocks the door to success in marriage is the third person of the Covenant. As scripture for this chapter reminds us, "Husband and wife, be subject to one another out of reverence for Christ." We are equipped to be our best for each other in marriage by desiring His presence, seeking His guidance, communing with Him in daily prayer, striving for His empowering Love and Grace, and rejoicing in Him always as Philippians 4:7 invites Christians to do. In so doing, we free our marriage partner from the impossible role of being supernatural. Jesus Christ is the ever-present Lord. He is the only One who is perfect. We certainly are not. We therefore do not <u>expect</u> the other to provide the inner gifts and strengths of life that come only from Him.

CHAPTER FOUR

SACRED AS CHRIST AND THE CHURCH

Ephesians 5:22, 25-33, *"Wives, be subject to your husbands as you are to the Lord. Husbands, love your wives, just as Christ loved the Church and gave Himself up for her, in order to make her holy by cleansing her with the washing of water by the word, so as to present the Church to Himself in splendor, without spot or wrinkle or anything of the kind –yes, so that she may be holy and without blemish. In the same way, husbands should love their wives as they do their own bodies. He who loves his wife loves himself. For no one ever hates his own body, but he nourishes and tenderly cares for it, just as Christ does for the Church, because we are members of His Body. For this reason a man will leave his father and mother and be joined to his wife, and the two will become one flesh. This is a great mystery, and I am applying it to Christ and the Church. Each of you, however, should love his wife as himself, and a wife should respect her husband."*

Many couples are surprised to hear marriage compared to religion or with some reference to God. Yet there isn't any subject more central to the very life of marriage than God.

One example of this is the couple who got a divorce over religion. The wife explained that religion was the only problem they had in their two years of marriage. She said, "He thought he was God, and I didn't."

Scripture leads us to believe that God is the source of our very being, and the One who designed marriage for man and woman. Psalm 100 declares, "Know that the Lord is God. It is He that made us, and we are His; we are His people, and the sheep of His pasture...For the Lord is good; His steadfast love endures forever, and His faithfulness to all generations."

Do you see the connection of God and marriage? It is God who made us male and female. It is God who gave us the supreme gift of marriage. It is God whose steadfast love endures forever. It is God's faithfulness that sustains us throughout all generations. We therefore need God to have a love that is steadfast and enduring. We need God's faithfulness to have the will and strength to be faithful to the one we marry. When we put ourselves in God's place and rely on our own resources to make marriage work, we always come up short. We may continue to live together with some contractual agreements, but without God, we will never experience the oneness that completes a man and woman.

After explaining the sacred terms of marriage, Paul says in Ephesians 5:32, "This is a great mystery." We all spontaneously respond with agreement: "Marriage is a great mystery." Yet, when we trust God with all our heart and do not rely on our own insights, and when we acknowledge Him in all our ways, He "makes straight our paths," as Proverbs 3:3-5 reminds us.

All couples want to walk together on paths that lead straight to love, happiness, and meaningful purposes. God is the One who can make this our destiny. The most important decision a couple can make for the success of their future is the promise to acknowledge God as the Lord of their lives. By daily seeking His Will and Way above their own, they will discover that through their best efforts and responsible living, God will provide all they need for a lasting marriage.

It is essential to understand that this is not about religion. It is about the True and Living God. God does not call us to religion. He calls us to Himself. God does not decree that we be religious. He desires a personal relationship with each of us now and for eternity. Religion is only humanity's attempt to become acceptable to the gods of personal belief. All religions and cults (and there are thousands of them in the world today) have their belief systems, rituals, rules and regulations. But they are all alike and equal in being powerless to forgive sin, restore righteousness, bridge the chasm between people and the God of their creation, and defeat death in order to have eternal life. God alone can accomplish all of this. Religions, cults, and human philosophies never have and never will. It is good to be tolerant and admit that all religions are equal. But it is wise to know that there is only One True God who loves us and has the Power to restore us to His original purpose of loving relationships.

Yes, we each are created in God's Image. But human sin and selfishness blur God's image, and cause us to abandon God's Will and Purpose. The result is separation, alienation, discord, divorce, and death. Marriage

32

for a man and woman that originally reflects the very nature of God and His righteousness becomes reduced to mutual exploitation. Instead of honoring and cherishing each other in marriage, the story of Adam and Eve in Genesis 3 states that after they disobeyed God's Will, they began blaming and accusing each other. This is how sin operates! It takes what is intended to be pure and lovely, and corrupts it into hostility and disappointment. Paul says in Romans 3:22 – 23, "...For there is no distinction, since all have sinned and fall short of the Glory of God." He then asks in Romans 6:21, "So what advantage did you then get from the things of which you now are ashamed? The end of those things is death."

God, however, will not be defeated by human sin and the corruption of marriage. God who is Eternal Love acts to undo the results of our fallen nature. God does what religion can never do. God established a "covenant" with the Hebrew people which is understood in the Old Testament as a "marriage relationship." God promises to bless His people <u>if they will be faithful</u> to His Will and Laws. By their faithfulness, God counted them as righteous, as stated in Genesis 15:6. God promised The Messiah "who will come" and live on earth a perfect and pure life. He will undo the results of sin by offering His life as the sacrifice death requires from all who have fallen short of the Glory of God.

Jesus Christ is the One who fulfills the marriage covenant God established with the Hebrew people by living in perfect righteousness for the Glory of God. He is the One who atones for the sins of the world by giving His life on the Cross in absolute love. Although He died for the sins of humanity, He alone was without sin. Death could not hold Him in the grave because of His righteousness. Death has no authority over one who never sinned. God therefore raised Jesus up from the grave on a Sunday morning that we now call Easter Day.

Jesus lives as the Savior of the world. All authority in heaven and earth has been given to Him, as stated in the Gospel of Matthew 28:18. Everyone who confesses Him as their Lord and Savior receives eternal forgiveness and God's everlasting love and grace. John 3:16 beautifully states this Good News by saying, "For God so loved the world that He gave His only Son, so that everyone who believes in Him may not perish but may have eternal life." All who accept God's gift and repent of sin are children of God. We become members of God's redeemed family: the Church, the "bride" of Jesus Christ. The Church, like the Covenant God made with the Hebrew people, is also understood as a marriage relationship. The Church <u>is</u> the Bride of Jesus Christ, and He is the Groom. In referring to Jesus, John the Baptist said, "He who has the bride is the bridegroom. The friend of the bridegroom, who stands and hears Him rejoices greatly at the bridegroom's voice. For this reason my joy has been fulfilled." (John 3:29 -30) The vision of John in Revelation 21: 2-4 also speaks in the language of marriage concerning Christ and the Church: "And I saw the holy city, the new Jerusalem, coming down out of heaven from God, prepared as a bride adorned for her husband. And I heard a loud voice from the throne saying, 'See, the home of God is among men and women. He will dwell with them as their God; they will be His peoples, and God Himself will be with them; He will wipe every tear from their eyes. Death will be no more, for the first things have passed away.'"

The one thing that stands out in the Mighty Acts of God's redemption of fallen humanity is the sacredness of marriage. Marriage is God's first gift to man and woman. Marriage is God's relationship with Israel for righteous living. Marriage is the New Covenant in Jesus Christ with the Church. And the relationship of a husband and wife is restored to the sacredness of marriage when Jesus Christ is honored as Savior and Lord, as Ephesians 5:21 affirms.

In this Biblical context regarding the sacredness of marriage, there are three guiding principles for a husband and wife: (1) Jesus Christ is the model for true love that completes human life. (2) A wife is to be subject to her husband as to the Lord. (3) A husband is to love his wife just as Christ loved the Church and gave Himself up for her.

FIRST, Jesus Christ is our model for unselfish love. He values every person with His Divine Perspective. He alone sees each one as an original creation by God the Father. He glorifies God by loving people regardless of their condition or position in life. His love transcends every wrong, every mask, and every act of rebellion. His acceptance of people for the possibility of their redemption and salvation is unconditional. His willingness to forgive and restore broken relationships is unequaled in human history. His love is perfect, self giving, and always in the best interest of others. Although Jesus Christ had many enemies, no one ever accused Him of being selfish, dishonest, or deceiving. He taught and practiced the highest standard of righteousness, and always forgave those who did wrong to Him.

He is the very incarnation of True Love that has the power to enable us to love as we have been loved. When a man and woman in the sacred bond of marriage say they love each other, their love is informed and enabled by the Love of Jesus Christ. This love is "gift love" which is freely given without expectations and conditions attached. It is not "need love" that is based on self serving principles such as "I will love you as long as you meet my needs."

SECOND, a wife is to be subject to her husband as to the Lord. She understands that Jesus Christ is the One of history who restored women to their rightful position of equality with the value of men. Jesus affirmed women in His teaching and ministry by respecting them, defending them, and entrusting them with the Good News of His resurrection. It was women who came first to the open tomb on Easter morning to learn that their Lord had conquered death. Women were the first to tell others that Jesus Christ is truly the Resurrected Savior of the world! Jesus, therefore, released women from the bondage of Jewish law that declared them the sole "property" of their fathers and husbands. Jesus overturned the Greek and Roman culture that denied women equal opportunity and respect as men enjoyed. If women had no other reason to honor Jesus Christ and hold Him in reverence, this one act of their liberation would be more than enough to justify their allegiance to Him. Wives who know Jesus in this way, and who have experienced His love, are able to respect their husbands by being subject to them as to the Lord.

THIRD, the guiding principle for the sacred covenant of marriage is for husbands to love their wives as Christ loved the Church and gave Himself up for her. The husband who is redeemed and forgiven by the love of Jesus Christ is able to love his wife with unselfish devotion. He is accountable to the Lord to have integrity, faithfulness, and wisdom. His wife is therefore able to trust him, respect him, and be subject to him for she knows he seeks her highest good in all that he does. He endeavors to grow spiritually and live a life of holiness so he can lead his wife to be holy and without blemish as Christ has done for the Church. The husband provides loving leadership in marriage, not to control and dominate, but to voluntarily give his best in maintaining a home of peace, joy, forgiveness, and security. His role as leader resembles the way Christ serves the Church. It is always unselfish, joyful, and for the Glory of God. It is no wonder then that a wife can respect, honor, and cherish her husband who serves her in these ways.

When couples live by these principles, the bedroom is often the place where the sacredness of their marriage is realized the most. Although it is personal for me to discuss our times of intimacy, Sandra and I experience love in the bedroom as an incredible gift from heaven. Our very souls touch with fulfillment in the rich and joyful sharing of passion for each other. Those times are like pure worship when we feel so very close to God. In the moment of ecstasy the predominant feeling is gratitude. Only God could make such a wonderful experience as this possible. We feel so thankful for God's gifts of life, love, and marriage. We then understand more clearly why God uses the analogy of the Church as being the Bride of Jesus Christ. In our love making, God wants us to catch a glimpse of His Love being so much greater than the love we could ever share in marriage. Some people like to say they feel the closest to God in nature. The beauty and wonder of nature do reflect the Glory of God as Psalm 8 and 19 declare. Yet, nature alone does not communicate God's love. Remember, nature is also violent and destructive — think about snakes, lions, grizzly bears, earthquakes, avalanches, and tornadoes. It is the sacredness of marriage and the relationships of love that draw us to the attributes of God's Love, Grace, and Joy more than nature, fame, and fortune.

Marriage and the Church, therefore, are the institutions through which God is at work, restoring His creation to holy living. The indwelling of the Holy Spirit enables people who are baptized in Christ to live free from selfishness, hostility, divorce, and death. Just as God loves us, we now are able to love with Divine Love that the world cannot give or take from us. We are able to forgive as we have been forgiven. We can live in peace, joy, and hope because Jesus Christ is <u>with</u> us. Marriage can and should be sacred as Christ and His Bride, the Church, are sacred. Our promises to "love, honor, cherish, and be faithful until death separates us" can be realized in God's gift of marriage. This is so because there are <u>three</u> now in the Covenant of marriage, instead of the limited two in the "contract" of marriage that our fallen world offers.

CHAPTER FIVE

LEAVING, CLEAVING, AND BECOMING

Mark 10: 6-9, Jesus said, *"From the beginning of creation, 'God made them male and female. For this reason a man shall leave his father and mother and cleave to his wife, and the two shall become one flesh.' So they are no longer two, but one flesh. Therefore what God has joined together, let no one separate."*

The transition from being a single person to a partner in marriage involves Leaving, Cleaving, and Becoming. For many individuals, **Leaving** is the hardest step.

Samantha is a good example of this process. Her father at the wedding escorted her down the aisle of the Church to where the groom was standing by the minister. The minister asked, "Who gives this woman to be married to this man?" Her father turning toward the congregation said, "All of you know this is Samantha's third marriage. I am here to give her away again. I will continue to give her away until someone is able to keep her from coming back home!"

In Jesus' teaching about marriage, he explains that it is necessary to leave father and mother when you become a husband and wife. This is not a violation of the Fifth Commandment which, according to Exodus 20:12, is to "Honor your father and mother." It is the duty a son and daughter are to fulfill as long as their parents live. But marriage shifts "first place" from parents to each other. Jesus is saying that when it is <u>time</u> for a man and woman to marry, they are to transfer their first allegiance from their childhood home to the new home they are establishing. They are to do this as lovingly and positively as possible, but do it they must. They are to depend on their parents no longer for emotional support and fulfillment. They are to look to each other for this satisfaction. They are to become responsible for their financial needs, and not expect their parents to provide for them. They are to prioritize their time and activities around each other, and include parents and other family members in their secondary planning.

For example, special times of the year like Thanksgiving, Christmas, New Year's Day, Easter, Fourth of July, and birthdays can't be celebrated in three or four different family settings at the same time. Even though a couple would enjoy being with everyone on these occasions, it is not possible. Choices have to be made. Some of the old traditions must give way to new ones that fit the lifestyle of the newly married couple. The couple needs the freedom from parents and family to decide what is best for their marriage and home. Parents need to give their blessing to their son and daughter when marriage takes place so they can be free to honor each other with first place without feeling guilty of neglecting them. Plans to alternate getting together from year to year with the different families are effective ways of maintaining the ties that are important to relatives. It takes unselfish hearts and a great deal of patience for such plans to succeed. But as long as the wife knows she is first with her husband, and he knows this is true with his wife, marriage can remain positive and happy. Even when family members do not cooperate as they should, the married couple can be at peace within themselves knowing they are following our Lord's direction in "Leaving."

Some years ago while serving a Church as Senior Pastor, a very unhappy young woman came to my study to discuss her situation. She told me of her story of getting married to a wonderful man seven years ago. They each had loving and supportive parents. Their first year together in a downtown apartment was wonderful. They both were working to save money for a down payment on a house they wanted to buy. In the second year of marriage his father died unexpectedly. His mother asked that they move in with her as she adjusted to life without her husband. They agreed to do so because it would not only be of comfort to his mother, but it would also help them save even more money for a house of their own. As I carefully listened to her, I was trying to figure out what the problem was.

She went on to say, "We have been in his mother's home now for six years. Whenever she wants time with him, I am always put in second place. We want to have a baby, but he says, 'It isn't possible until mother is able to live by herself.' I have asked him many times when will we use the money we saved to buy our own home. His answer is, 'You know we can't leave mother yet.'" She then looked at me with tears streaming from her eyes and asked, "Am I being selfish to want to have my own home?"

It took me time to answer her for I wanted to be respectful to all concerned. But my response was the words of Jesus, "For this reason a man shall leave his father and mother and cleave to his wife, and the two shall become one flesh." I made the observation that her husband obviously did <u>not</u> leave his mother when they married in order to be one with her. He did not make the transfer of first loyalty from his mother to his wife. "Yes indeed," I said. "The two of you were right to provide immediate support, compassion, and help to this grieving mother. But you were wrong to do it at the expense of your marriage and home. God would have you find a way to do both without sacrificing the other." After a prayer together, she left my study with renewed confidence to reclaim her marriage. I promised to be of help in every way I could as long as the terms of God's plan for marriage were honored.

During the wedding ceremony the process of leaving is openly affirmed when the question is asked, "Who presents this woman to be married to this man?" The word "presents" is used instead of "gives." Give indicates ownership, and a woman is not "owned" by her family or husband. The father (sometimes it is necessary for another family member to take his place) usually makes the "presentation" by placing the hand of the bride in the hand of the groom. He then steps back and is seated.

The groom moves to the bride's side, taking the place of the father. Hopefully the bride will always love and respect her father. But once the father places her hand in the groom's hand and steps back, the bride from that time forward looks to her husband for the care her father has provided. For example, it is the duty and privilege of the father from her birth until she is married to provide protection and the necessities of life. The father serves as the spiritual leader of the home for true worship of God and the teaching of God's Truth for right living. Now it is the husband who is to be her protector, provider, spiritual leader, and encourager for her to develop her full potential as a woman. She is to be his helper as God planned in the beginning, and to provide the gifts of nurturing of their relationship and family. Together they become partners, lovers, and best friends. Leaving is essential for this to happen.

After leaving and making the transition from parents, the next step toward becoming husband and wife is to **Cleave**. Jesus restates God's purpose for marriage with stunning clarity. God's plan is for marriage to be lifelong faithfulness. The word "cleave" means to be joined, to adhere, and to be faithful. It implies, as the words say in a marriage ceremony,

"Forsaking all others, keep yourself only to each other as long as you both shall live." God's Word in Hebrews 13:4 magnifies this intent by saying, "Let marriage be held in honor by all, and let the marriage bed be kept undefiled." Marriage is joining a man and woman together in a bond of togetherness. The promises they make to each other and to God are the cords that bind them as lovers, partners, and best friends until death separates them. The Blessing of God upon their union breathes sustaining life into their oneness. Literally a husband and wife are joined together as "one flesh." In the act of consecration, their lives are now shared as "we" and "us" and "our." The former yearning for fulfillment as expressed by the pronouns "I" and "me" and "mine" is satisfied with the new beginning and promising future that marriage provides.

The goal of leaving and cleaving is **Becoming**. Life is a wonderful gift of God. But there is a future dimension for each life that completes it with even greater value. It is the experience of becoming husband and wife. As we remember from Genesis 2:18, "The Lord God said, 'it is not good that the man should be alone. I will make him a helper as his partner.'" This is God's original purpose for human life, and deep within each heart is the yearning for wholeness. However, our fallen world has shattered this divine plan. For many men and women marriage never happens. For many others the vows of oneness are not kept. The self-centered forces of secular society, the gods of materialism, the instability of home life, and the increasing mobility of contemporary life styles all undermine the sanctity of marriage. Yet, the faint memory of God's divine plan at creation and the secret hope of human hearts cause us to seek this "Becoming."

Even in this fallen world the good news is we still can "Become." II Corinthians 5:17-18 assures us, "So if anyone is in Christ, there is a new creation: everything old has passed away; see, everything has become new! All this is from God, who reconciled us to Himself through Christ." Marriage can be fulfilling and joyful when we enter God's plan of marriage and follow the steps God gives us for success.

As a couple and I were discussing these steps of Leaving, Cleaving, and Becoming in preparation for their wedding ceremony, the bride asked, "Isn't this what the Unity Candle is all about?" I happily said, "Absolutely! Even if we don't include the Unity Candle in the service, it is essential that the two of you take these three important steps."

The Unity Candle is a visual representation of Leaving, Cleaving, and Becoming. When appropriate, it is meaningful for the mothers to participate. As they are escorted to their seats at the beginning of the wedding ceremony, they approach the Unity Candle and light the side candles. This indicates the love and blessings given to the marriage from the groom's family and the bride's family. It also is a public acknowledgement of parents "releasing" the son and daughter from their authority to the freedom they will need to become husband and wife. This also means in a humorous way that the parents aren't responsible for their bills any more. Once marriage begins, the couple is to work and provide for their own living expenses without being dependent on their parents.

During the wedding ceremony, usually after the vows and rings have been exchanged, the couple lifts the candles their mothers have lighted. Together they light the Unity Candle — which is the one in the center. They return the two side candles to their places without blowing out the flame. Three candles are now burning. The one in the center symbolizes their Unity in Marriage and the <u>new</u> home they are establishing. The two side candles represent the two homes from which they come. The light and warmth of the three flames are to remind everyone present of the continuing love, respect, and encouragement the three homes will seek to provide for each other.

Sometimes a couple mistakenly assumes that the two side candles represent the bride and groom. After they light the center candle, they blow out the other two indicating they have become one, and are no longer two. This is not correct! They always will be the separate and unique persons God designed them to be. Following their parents' example, marriage is the means of "Becoming" husband and wife by joining together to start a new home and family. The three candles rightfully represent the parents' blessings, and the couple's promises to be faithful to each other as long as they live with God's enabling Spirit.

CHAPTER SIX

THE ENDURING FOUNDATION

Matthew 7: 24–27, *"Everyone then who hears these words of mine and does them will be like a wise man who built his house on rock. The rain fell, the floods came, and the winds blew and beat on that house, but it did not fall, because it had been founded on rock. And everyone who hears these words of mine and does not do them will be like a foolish man who built his house on sand. The rain fell, and the floods came, and the winds blew and beat against that house, and it fell – and great was its fall."*

Four married guys were out golfing one Saturday morning. During their walk to the second hole, the following conversation ensued. The first guy said, "Man, you have no idea what I had to promise my wife so she wouldn't be angry about my playing golf today. I had to agree to clean out the entire garage when I get home this afternoon."

The second guy said, "That's nothing. I had to promise to take my wife out to the most expensive restaurant in town this evening. It will cost me a fortune." The third guy reported his getting away for the day wasn't easy either. He said, "I was supposed to paint the kitchen for my wife today. But she agreed for me to do it next weekend if I promised to paint the den as well."

They continued to play the third hole when they realized the fourth guy had not said a word. So they asked him, "What about you? We know your wife. She is tougher than any of ours." He replied, "I don't want to talk about it. Let's just say the foundation for the new house will be poured next Tuesday."

In building a new house, the fourth golfer at least knew the foundation was the starting point! Jesus would agree. His parable about the two builders in the Gospel of Matthew 7: 24-27 teaches us that a foundation has to be strong and secure in good and bad times for a dwelling to withstand the storms and difficulties of life. In His "Sermon On The Mount" (Matthew 5, 6, and 7), Jesus gives us the blueprint for a stable foundation on which one can build a balanced life, a stable home, and a happy marriage. This is the greatest teaching the world has ever received. Jesus, the only One in human history who lived a perfect and holy life, knows what He is talking about: "Everyone then who hears these words of mine and does them will be like a wise man..."

This is especially true for any couple beginning a marriage. They are never wiser than when they hear and do what Jesus teaches. In order to have a foundation on which to build and develop a successful, happy, and fulfilling marriage, Jesus' blueprint from The Sermon On The Mount proves to be a trustworthy guide. He makes it clear that a "rock solid foundation" is the wise choice. I believe there are four key principles in His teaching that constitute the four corners of the marital foundation.

The first corner of this foundation is commonly called "The Golden Rule." In Matthew 7:12, Jesus says, "In everything, do to others as you would have them do to you." I believe, and have found it to be true in my marriage, that there is no greater gift a husband and wife can give each other than the promise to always live by the Golden Rule. This means that from your wedding day and for the rest of your lives, you will do your best to <u>care</u> for each other, <u>treat</u> each other, and <u>speak</u> to each other according to what you would want and appreciate. If couples would make this the corner stone of their marriage and home, I am convinced they would avoid at least seventy five percent of all the problems they would otherwise have. Instead of disappointments, they would mutually benefit from the blessings of unselfish love and kindness just by doing for each other what each would want the other to do. If couples would start out their marriage by hearing and doing this one teaching from Jesus' Sermon on the Mount, I further believe the majority of divorces in the world would be avoided. Reciprocal love would result in lasting and stable homes.

I have tried each day of my marriage to say to Sandra "I love you." Although my love is genuine, some of my motivation comes from Jesus' Golden Rule, because I want her to love me. Countless times she has done thoughtful and unexpected things for me which in turn cause me to want to do more for her. When Sandra broke her ankle from a fall in her garden, the six weeks of care were a real test of my resolve to do for her as I would want her to do for me. At the moment when frustration was coming to the surface, I quickly imagined how it would be if <u>my</u> ankle was broken. Without a doubt, I knew she would lovingly provide every assistance she could during my recovery. Therefore, I was eager to unselfishly be there for her as best I could. Over and over again, we have proven that this one principle works for our mutual good in strengthening our marriage.

The second corner of the foundation of marriage according to Jesus' Sermon on the Mount is His teaching "to go the second mile for each other" (Matthew 5:41). The legal and worldly contract for marriage only requires a couple to go so-called one mile or "equal" distances for each other. This is what we know to be the 50/50 proposition. The husband is to give 50% toward the marriage, and the wife is to give 50%. The plan is to meet in the middle, and consider everything equal. The problem comes when one doesn't deliver his or her 50%. The other normally reacts with an unwilling attitude or withholds their 50%. Conflict and disappointment result. If it continues into separation and then divorce, the Judge at the divorce hearing rules that all assets and properties are to be divided equally. According to their contract, all they brought to the marriage was 50% each, and all they can take from it is "their 50%." This arrangement is a very inadequate corner for a strong and stable foundation needed for a happy and lasting marriage.

Jesus says going one mile is never enough. He teaches us "to go the second mile for each other." This means that the Covenant of Marriage sets the goal at 100% effort for a husband and wife to invest in their marriage for each other. No one is perfect and there will be many times when only 60%, 70%, or 80% can be given. But even in so doing when the goal is 100%, far more will be given and received than in the "contract of marriage" with a goal of 50%. Jesus makes it clear that the 50/50 agreement doesn't work for building a durable foundation on which to live.

His plan is quite amazing. When a couple is wise and endeavors to "go the second mile" for each other, they have the possibility of enjoying all the benefits that each brings to the marriage. On the day of marriage, the wife promises to give all that she is and has for the highest good of her husband. He also promises to give to her all that he is and has for her fulfillment. God blesses this Covenant of unselfish love, and permits each to have the full measure of their investment. No longer does the couple think and talk in terms of "what is mine" and what is "yours". Instead, their new life together is built upon the awareness that everything is "ours." The more each one invests in the marriage, the more both receive.

If they each strive to give 100% to each other and with God providing His 100% of love, wisdom, and care, they can have it all! This is what we all seek. Our Lord teaches us how to have the <u>foundation</u> on which marriage grows with lasting fulfillment.

The third corner that Jesus gives for a secure foundation are Jesus' words, "Always tell the truth." He says in Matthew 5:37, "Let your 'Yes' be Yes, and your 'No' be No." In other words, Jesus is simply saying, "Always be honest and clear in what you say." Be trustworthy. Especially in marriage and with your family, be truthful. Wear integrity upon your breast as your medal of honor.

This is so essential for marriage to be healthy. A husband and wife are to trust each other because they are committed to telling the truth. They <u>are</u> each other's best friend. The most intimate person in a husband's life is his wife, and her soul mate is her husband. The channel of honesty must always be open so meaningful communication can flow with confidence in each other.

Beginning on the day of marriage, there should be no secrets between a husband and wife. It is not necessary to tell each other the secrets before marriage. This could be embarrassing, if not dangerous. But once the commitment to the covenant of marriage is made, the two lives are to be transparent. Everything that is relevant in their relationship is to be open and clear. There is to be no cover-up or deception in marriage. If the husband wins the lottery jackpot, he is to share this good news with his wife and of course, the money. He is not to hoard it for himself. If the wife receives a double bonus at the end of year for her good work, she is to share this good fortune with her husband. All financial matters are to be in the open, and each deserves to be clearly informed of spending and income matters. A husband and wife, therefore, need to spend time and careful planning in making mutual decisions about all financial matters. In regard to other personal matters, a husband and wife are to always tell each other the truth even if it means enduring the adverse consequences of mistakes and bad decisions.

An important component of this corner of the marriage foundation is confidentiality. As best friends, married partners are to respect each other's personal matters. Such information is not to be shared with relatives, friends, or colleagues at work without permission. You are to share with each other the hurts and hopes of life with mutual trust that confidentiality will be maintained. This is clearly a matter of being <u>honest</u> with the one you have promised to love, honor, and cherish for as long as you both shall live.

The fourth corner of the marriage foundation is Jesus' word, "Forgive." He says in Matthew 6:14-15, "For if you forgive others their trespasses, your heavenly Father will also forgive you; but if you do not forgive others, neither will your Father forgive your trespasses." Beginning on your wedding day and throughout your journey of marriage, promise to forgive each other and yourself when mistakes occur and wrongs are done. In marriage, you will disappoint each other. You will do and say things that are hurtful. But by God's Grace, you can talk and work through your misunderstandings and thus forgive each other.

You can be reconciled with each other by genuinely confessing your wrongs and offering true forgiveness as God forgives. Do not allow your hurt feelings and broken pride to determine your relationship with your husband or wife. When problems develop, seek God's forgiving love to bring healing and a new beginning. God through Jesus Christ is the central person of the Covenant of Marriage. The success of your marriage doesn't depend just on the two of you. Let God guide you with humility, understanding, and Grace to compromise when necessary. Always be willing to forgive when the other is honest in admitting wrong.

Some years ago a woman called to tell me she and her husband were separated. It had been two years since I performed their wedding ceremony. She said he had been unfaithful and had participated in an affair with a woman he met at work. She was devastated, and understandably angry. At the end of our phone conversation, I suggested that she ask her husband to call me. After a few days had passed, he called and made an appointment with me. During our conversation, he accepted full responsibility of his infidelity. He had ended the affair, and desperately wanted to repair their marriage. I asked him to try and verbalize the feelings his wife was experiencing. I wanted him to hear his words describe the shame and feelings of rejection that his wife was experiencing because of his unfaithfulness. It was an emotional time for him. The only hope and encouragement I could offer were the words of Jesus that <u>promise</u> God's forgiveness when we repent.

Several months later, his wife called to tell me the amazing story of their reconciliation. She said he called one evening and asked if he could come over to talk. She was cold to the idea, but agreed for him to come. Their conversation about work and recent activities was awkward, but polite. Then, with deep emotion, he confessed to betraying her. He made no effort to defend his unfaithfulness, or excuse his behavior. He simply asked if she would drink from their wedding chalice with him. He reminded her that during their wedding ceremony when they received

Holy Communion, the cup was presented to them as a symbol of God's Promise to <u>always be with them</u>. It was a visible sign that God would never let a problem come their way that His Love, Grace, and Power could not overcome through their love, faith, and forgiveness.

He asked her if she would drink again from their chalice and call upon God to give her the Grace to forgive him. He told her that he didn't deserve forgiveness. He also knew that she could not without God's help give him another chance. But he loved her with all his heart. He wanted to experience her forgiveness so he could do his best to heal the hurt he had caused her.

She told me this request was a total surprise. Without any words spoken, she went to the china cabinet and took down their wedding chalice. He opened a bottle of red wine from the kitchen. He poured wine into the cup with tears as he asked her to forgive him. Together they drank from this symbol of Covenant with each other and with God, tasting their salty tears more than the sweet wine. As they embraced, he said a short prayer. All she could say was, "I will need some time." He left her alone that evening with some lingering hope.

Several weeks passed with more conversations, shared meals, and two counseling sessions with a Christian psychologist. They agreed for him to move back into their house. She wanted me to know that God's Grace did what she never could have done alone. She forgave him! The foundation of their marriage held. They were reconciled. Love and Hope and Joy returned. The last time I heard from them was when they announced the birth of their second child. The return of their investment in a Godly marriage proved to be worth all the effort and pain they experienced.

Jesus Christ is the architect who gives us the blueprint for a strong foundation. If we are wise to hear and do His words, we will make sure the corners of the rock on which we build our marriage and home are:

1) The Golden Rule
2) Going the second mile for each other
3) Always being honest
4) Forgiving each other by the Grace of God.

The other teachings of our Lord in His Sermon on the Mount are like stone slabs that lay across these corners that establish a solid foundation. Read them in the Gospel of Matthew, chapters 5, 6, and 7. They are more valuable for a happy and lasting marriage than wealth and fame.

CHAPTER SEVEN

LOVE WITH STAYING POWER

I Corinthians 13: 4 – 8a; 13, *"Love is patient; love is kind; love is not envious or boastful or arrogant or rude. It does not insist on its own way; it is not irritable or resentful; it does not rejoice in wrongdoing, but rejoices in the truth. It bears all things, believes all things, hopes all things, endures all things. Love never ends...and now faith, hope, and love abide, these three; and the greatest of these is love."*

W e were all created from love and for love by God, who is the very essence of love. We yearn to love and be loved as a flower seeks water to live. Love is the primary goal of marriage.

Henry and Carol illustrate this yearning. They were snuggling in his Dad's parked car one spring evening. It was a romantic moment with the full moon shining across the lake. He was finally able to say the words he had been rehearsing in his thoughts for some time: "Carol, I love you." Before she could respond he continued to say, "Now I know I can't provide you with a new car and fancy things like Jack Green can. I'm not as good looking and popular as he is. I know I'm not as talented and athletic as he is. But Carol, I really do love you." She was surprised by this declaration of affection. After a couple of moments of contemplation, she said, "Well Henry, why don't you tell me a little more about this Jack Green?"

We all need and want to be loved, but like Carol, sometimes we can be confused about what genuine love really is. True love has staying power. It endures in the good and difficult times of life. It never ends. Just where do we get this kind of love? Some say this love comes from the passionate feelings that you experience for someone who attracts you. Others say true love is a decision. God says true and fulfilling love is a gift. God is the giver, and He provides the heavenly treasure we call "Love." This love that our hearts desire comes uniquely from God. I John 4:16 clearly states that "God is love, and those who abide in love abide in God, and God abides in them."

The Apostle Paul identifies God's gift of love in I Corinthians 13 by using the Greek word "Agape." It specifically refers to divine love. He could have used *Phileo* which means tender affection that friends have for each other. He could have chosen the word *Eros* which is the Greek word for sexual passion. He also avoided using the Greek word *Philanthropos* which means humanitarian kindness and compassion for others. The Greek word *Storge* is the love family members have for each other, but even this word was not adequate for God's Love. Paul knew through the inspiration of the Holy Spirit that the only word big enough to communicate divine love is "Agape." This is the love God generously gives to us through our faith in Him for our salvation.

It is also the love God provides for us to share with our mate in the Covenant of Marriage. It alone has the staying power to enable us to fulfill our marriage vows "to be faithful in plenty and in want; in joy and in sorrow; in sickness and in health; as long as we both shall live; according to God's Holy Ordinance." Feel good love can never stay the course. Sexual love is too changeable to complete the journey of marriage. Selfish love is too weak to fulfill the promises made on our wedding day. Only "Agape" love bears all things, believes all things, hopes all things, endures all things, and never ends. We, therefore, should make sure God's name is the first one on our wedding guest list. If invited, God will bring the greatest gift for marriage we could ever receive! His gift is "Agape." It will never wear out. It will never get old. It will never lose its power. It will last as long as a couple abides in God and keeps alive His priceless gift by sharing it with each other.

Just as Jesus gives us His words in the Sermon on the Mount for the foundation of our home, I believe Paul would say God's "Agape" love should be its roof. He beautifully explains the qualities of God's "Agape" in chapter 13 of I Corinthians that gives us joy and staying power in marriage. When I was a sophomore at Emory University, I remember the Professor of my English Literature class beginning our course of study by saying, "The greatest prose writing with depth and meaning in all human literature is I Corinthians 13." He said, "It is called the 'Love Chapter of The Bible.'" Since then, this great passage of the Bible has been the source of my understanding the nature of genuine love.

The number seven throughout the Bible represents that which is divine, and it is no coincidence that Paul names "seven aspects" of God's Love. They are patience, kindness, rejoicing in the truth, bearing all things, believing all things, hoping all things, and enduring all things.

In contrast to Agape, Paul list eight things that God's love is not. He says, "His Love is not envious or boastful or arrogant or rude. It does not insist on its own way; it is not irritable or resentful; and it does not rejoice in wrongdoing." Those who try to build their marriage and home on these self-serving conditions will soon discover that they are not adequate for a lasting relationship. They are like the unstable sand Jesus was talking about in His Sermon on the Mount.

However, wise couples who build their marriages on the Rock of Jesus Words with a sheltering roof of God's love will have secure homes. Such a roof can then display seven banners representing the qualities of "Agape."

THE FIRST BANNER OF LOVE IS PATIENCE. Is it surprising to you that this is the first quality of God's Love? Most young people would expect feelings, kissing, or excitement to be first. But those who are more mature are not surprised that patience is the first characteristic of real love. Husbands and wives especially understand that it takes a lot of patience to be married. Men and women are incredibly different. They have likes and dislikes that often clash. If they have true love for each other, they will temper their responses with patience when these differences surface.

Patience that comes from God's love enables us to control frustrations and seek compromises. It helps a husband accept the meticulous ways of his wife who knows exactly how she wants things done around the house. Patience enables a wife to endure her husband's procrastination with tasks he promised to accomplish on his day off. Patience "holds back" unnecessary corrections. Negative criticism and anger are the enemies of love. Patience is a "messenger" of love!

THE SECOND BANNER OF LOVE IS KINDNESS. It is often the little acts of kindness that mean the most in marriage. For a husband to prepare dinner when he knows his wife has experienced a frustrating day, to turn the TV off to give conversation an opportunity to convey feelings, and to provide a massage without being asked are thoughtful touches of kindness forever remembered with appreciation. When a wife anticipates her husband's needs for a business trip and packs his bag before he gets home from work, she demonstrates love's act of kindness. Kindness is also withholding words that would rebuke, correct, or cause hurt feelings.

There are many comments that are better unspoken than blurted out just to make a point. Love always seeks the other's highest good. Kindness is love's ambassador that promotes good will and positive attitudes.

Acts of kindness toward other people and even animals increase the respect a husband and wife have for each other. A husband who paid for a little boy's ice cream at the ball game when he didn't have enough money caused his wife to wink with satisfaction. The wife who prepared several meals for the neighbor who returned home from the hospital brought words of admiration from her husband. The couple who volunteers once a month at the animal shelter because the city is short on funds tells their friends that this is one of the best things they do together. The bond of marriage is strengthened with acts of kindness for each other as well as for anyone in need.

THE THIRD BANNER OF LOVE IS REJOICING IN THE TRUTH. It is very human to exaggerate the negatives about others and to comment on the mistakes people make. All of us have the tendency to justify ourselves or make ourselves seem better than we really are by pointing out the misdeeds of others. When husbands and wives do this to each other, their relationship suffers greatly. God gives us His love to rejoice in the truth. It teaches us to look for the good in each other instead of dwelling on their flaws and misdeeds. It means that because of our love we do not keep a "record" of wrongdoing. We try to deal with problems and misunderstandings with fairness and good communication. Then we apologize and forgive the wrongs. We don't make a list of each wrong for future ammunition when another fight occurs. Love guides us to rejoice in what is right and to celebrate what is true. We therefore can let go of the unpleasant experiences, and promote the positive attributes of marriage. God shows His love for us in this way by not remembering our sins once we sincerely confess them. He gives us this same love to work through our misunderstandings and to affirm each other with forgiveness and encouragement.

THE FOURTH BANNER OF LOVE IS BEARING ALL THINGS. Paul selects the Greek verb *"hupomenein"* to convey the dimension of love that continues to be faithful in the midst of adversity. The implication of this word is to cover the wrongs of others with the hope of forgiveness and reconciliation. Love seeks to keep confidential whenever possible the mistakes and shameful deeds of others until they can make things right again. This love helps them "save face" and maintain their dignity.

Bearing all things with "Agape" isn't passive resignation. Rather it is an active love that doesn't surrender to defeat. It continues to seek the solution to a problem, to make a positive out of a negative, and to strive toward a victory. It is the spirit of togetherness that a couple has when they are confident of God's empowering Presence even in the worst of times.

It is an awesome commitment for a man and woman to promise each other before God and those present at their wedding "to be faithful and loving in plenty and want; in joy and in sorrow; in sickness and in health; as long as we both shall live." Yet, they are able to be courageous in beginning this journey since God promises to be with them and provide "Agape" for their every need.

George Matheson, who wrote many beautiful hymns, illustrates this love that bears all things. He lost his vision, and the woman he loved left him and turned to another. Although the hurt of rejection and the agony of blindness were almost more than he could take, he wrote a prayer that expressed his faith in God whose "Agape" would be sufficient for all his needs. He said, "Not with dumb resignation, but with holy joy; not only with the absence of murmur, but with a song of praise." He promised to continue to fulfill God's Will no matter what he had to bear. Married couples in Christ also learn to depend on this staying power of God's love.

THE FIFTH BANNER OF LOVE IS BELIEVING IN ALL THINGS. Love takes God at His Word. The promises of God through Jesus Christ are dependable. God promises to forgive us our mistakes when we confess them. He then promises to give us Grace to forgive others who do us wrong! Believing in God's Word in this way results in Agape that enables us to give others the benefit of the doubt. We can overcome our suspicious and jealous nature and see the potential for good in the people closest to us. When we believe in the goodness of others, they more likely will seek to be good and do the right thing. In marriage, we bring out the best in each other when we expect the best, when we are quick to appreciate thoughtful acts, and when we trust each other. Goethe, a German poet, once said, "Treat a man as he appears to be, and you make him worse. But treat a man as if he were what he potentially could be, and you make him what he should be." Like the woman caught in adultery, Jesus treated her not as she was, but as she could become. His "Agape" always reaches out to each of us in this way. We too can believe all things good through His love.

I believe Paul had this in mind when he wrote to the Christians in Philippi, "Whatever is honorable, whatever is just, whatever is pure, whatever is pleasing, whatever is commendable, if there is any excellence and if there is anything worthy of praise, think about these things" (Philippians 4:8-9). Wouldn't you like to live with someone who thought and acted this way? Wouldn't you like to be this kind of person? The truth is all of us can with God's Love.

THE SIXTH BANNER OF LOVE IS HOPING ALL THINGS. Marriage begins with hope. It is a journey of hope. This banner can wave with confidence from the roof of a Christian home if hope comes from faith in God. Hope is more than dreams and wishful thoughts. Hebrews 11:1 declares, "Now faith is the assurance of things hoped for, the conviction of things not seen. " Through our faith, God promises His blessings of love, grace, joy, and peace. Our hope has reliability because God keeps His promises.

Paul increases our ability of hoping all things by saying, "Therefore, since we are justified by faith, we have peace with God through whom we have obtained access to this grace in which we stand; and we boast in our hope of sharing the glory of God...and hope does not disappoint us, because God's love has been poured into our hearts through the Holy Spirit that has been given to us" (Romans 5:1-2, 5).

Married couples will encounter one or more major challenges in their shared lives. They often struggle with bad habits, addictions, unemployment, accidents, health problems, tragedies in the lives of their children, and even infidelity. But faith in Jesus Christ keeps hope alive. God's love enables us to "hope all things." If both the husband and wife will continue believing, relying on the power of Agape, and doing the best they can, hope will see them to a solution. By hoping all things through Christ regardless of the situation, Paul says in Romans 8:37 – 39, we become "more than conquerors through Him who loves us. For I am convinced that neither death, nor life, nor angels, nor rulers, nor things present, nor things to come, nor powers, nor height, nor depth, nor anything else in all creation, will be able to separate us from the love of God in Christ Jesus our Lord."

THE SEVENTH BANNER OF LOVE IS ENDURING ALL THINGS. This banner is on the roof of a Christian home signaling to all within and without that "we will never give up." Surrender, divorce, and rejection are not an option. With God all things are possible. Like Paul in Philippians 4: 11-13, we can say, "I have learned to be content with whatever I have. I know what it is to have little, and I know what it is to have plenty...I can do all things through Him who strengthens me." God's love that is ours through faith is His gift to help us "keep on keeping on." The success of our marriage doesn't depend upon our love and efforts alone. God is with us. His power is sufficient for us to endure all things.

This is illustrated by the story of a young wife who had a facial tumor. Surgery was required. When she returned to her hospital room from the operating table, her husband stood at her side holding her hand. He couldn't help but notice the downward turn of her mouth on the left side of her face. The doctor was there and he gently explained a nerve had to be cut to remove the tumor. The husband asked, "Will it always be like this?" The doctor said, "Yes." He then said, "I think it is kinda cute." He then curved the right side of his lips to match hers. He leaned over and lovingly kissed her. She understood in the deepest way the meaning of Agape that enables a husband and wife to endure all things.

These seven banners of love from the roof top of our home not only signal the blessings of God, they remind us daily that God's love is sufficient for our every need. It is a great comfort to know that the success of our marriage does not depend just on our best efforts. It also depends on God's gift of love. God promises to provide a generous supply of love for us to share with each other every day. This love keeps us going, and gives us another chance when we fail. The more we live in God's love, the more we rejoice in His Presence and find fulfillment in our marriages.

A young bride wanted to give a great gift to her fiancé. She asked a sales woman in a fabric shop for some white material that would make a noisy and rustling sound. The woman brought out two bolts of fabric that she thought would fit the description, but couldn't help but ask, "Why would you want noisy fabric?" The young woman explained, "You see, I am getting married next month. My fiancé is blind. When I walk down the aisle of the church, I want him to hear me coming to be his wife."

This kind of love enables us to see the very image of God in His Gift of Marriage.

CHAPTER EIGHT

THE FOUR GOALS OF MARRIAGE

Philippians 3:13b-15a, *"This one thing I do: forgetting what lies behind and straining forward to what lies ahead, I press on toward the goal for the prize of the heavenly call of God in Christ Jesus. Let those of us then who are mature be of the same mind."*

In the scripture above, the apostle Paul emphasizes the importance of having a goal. He says be mature and forget what "lies behind you": continue to "press on" toward the goal set <u>before</u> you. His analogy is about an athlete who gives the race his best effort to achieve the prize. Marriage is a heavenly prize for it was conceived in the heart of God at the time of creation. It is a worthy goal for every couple.

One bride before her wedding had a goal in mind to make her marriage heavenly. As she was about to walk down the red carpet of the beautiful sanctuary, her eyes were fixed on three things. She saw the aisle before her, the white marble altar at the chancel of the Church, and the handsome man waiting by the minister to receive her hand. Her goal was clearly visible to her as she thought, "I'll alter him."

Although her goal was to change him to her liking, marriage cannot succeed on such a premise. No one is perfect, and all the "modifications" we try to impose on someone cannot overcome the differences we dislike. Marriage must have more noble goals than just "changing" our chosen mate.

After forty three years of marriage and performing almost twenty-two hundred weddings, I have come to believe that there are four great goals of marriage that every couple should seek with all their hearts.

During premarital counseling sessions, I encourage couples to write out the following goals with action steps beneath each one. The action steps are specific ways through which they will seek to accomplish each goal.

GOAL NUMBER ONE: WE WILL DO OUR BEST TO STAY PHYSICALLY FIT

1. We will exercise vigorously for at least thirty minutes four to five times a week.
2. We will eat healthy foods for good nutrition and energy.
3. We will never have more than two alcoholic drinks in four hours to remain sober and responsible for our actions.
4. We will help each other get seven or more hours of restful sleep every night.
5. We will get annual physical checkups to make sure we remain in good health.

This goal is first because we owe it to each other to be in the best physical condition possible. By doing so, we will have more energy to fulfill our responsibilities. We will be more playful and fun to live with every day. It will also help keep us healthy, avoiding illness and prolonging our lives. Perhaps one of the most important benefits of staying physically fit through the years is remaining attractive to each other during the cycles of aging.

GOAL NUMBER TWO: WE WILL DO OUR BEST TO STAY MENTALLY ALIVE

1. As best friends, we will learn new things together like dancing, singing, playing a musical instrument, speaking another language, and enjoying certain sporting activities. We will participate in seminars of special interests and take continuing education courses offered by Churches, community colleges, and other organizations.
2. We will start a hobby like gardening, bird watching, astronomy, photography, traveling, raising an animal, card playing, and other challenging games.
3. We will start a collection. There are many antique items to study and collect. Collecting is fun! Memorabilia and signatures of musicians, actors, sports figures, and politicians are not only interesting but sometimes valuable.

4. We will develop the art of communication, actively listening to each other and sharing feelings and ideas. Specific books, seminars, marriage retreats, and even counseling can be very helpful in these areas.
5. We will develop friendships with people who are younger, older, smarter, and more talented than we are just for the sake of learning and growing.

Staying mentally alive in marriage enables a couple to avoid boredom. They will continually be discovering new things about each other and the endless marvels of God's world and universe. The more a couple learns together, the more they will grow together as one. If they do not invest time and effort in learning together, they will surely grow apart.

GOAL NUMBER THREE: WE WILL DO OUR BEST TO STAY FINANCIALLY SECURE

1. We will give to God the full tithe — which is ten percent of our income — as scripture teaches in Malachi 3: 10, and as Jesus says we should do in Luke 11:42.
2. We will be honest and pay our taxes in full. Jesus tells us in Luke 20:25, we should render unto Caesar (the government) what is Caesars' (taxes), and unto God (the tithe) what is God's. Be wise and pay only the taxes that are required by law, but always live by the truth.
3. We will identify all debts we owe as a couple. We will keep no financial secrets from each other. We will develop a plan to pay against our debts until we fulfill God's Word in Romans 13:8 which says, "Owe no one anything but to love them." Count your house mortgage as an investment for you are paying it down each month. But other debts put a lending institution or another person in authority over your lives and home. God wants you to be in charge of your home with freedom to manage your personal affairs.
4. We will plan and write out a budget that realistically represents our incomes and expenses. We will exercise discipline and restraint in using our money and resources. We will maintain regular and positive communication with each other as to how our budget is working for us. We will remain committed to our agreements, and avoid being selfish, defensive, and dishonest. We will

be flexible and considerate when changes need to be made. We will seek financial counseling when we need help in revising our budget.

5.   In addition to the above plan for managing our money, we will begin a savings fund. Proverbs 13:11 says, "Wealth gained quickly is soon lost, but those who gather little by little increase their wealth." Money put aside for special occasions or for emergencies will increase our sense of financial security and peace of mind.

These five Biblical principles represent God's Plan for our financial security. God wants each of us to have the resources that meet our needs and add to the joy of our living. Through our responsible living and wise decisions, God will see that our money is a blessing to us and not a curse. Financial problems rank second among all the difficulties married couples experience. Most of these problems can be minimized or eliminated by faithfully practicing these five Biblical steps for managing our financial affairs.

GOAL NUMBER FOUR: WE WILL DO OUR BEST TO STAY SPIRITUALLY STRONG

1.   We will honor Jesus Christ as the central person of our covenant of marriage. This is God's Will according to Ephesians 5:21. Rejoice in the Lord always (Philippians 4: 4- 7), and look to Him for wisdom, strength, and peace. We will continually seek from Him Grace, Forgiveness, and Reconciliation with God and with each other as we need it.

2.   We will worship God regularly as a couple and family. We will join a community of faith and seek to contribute to the vitality of the congregation as much as we desire to be nurtured by its ministry.

3.   We will pray for each other daily. There is no greater act of love and consideration than to lift up each other before God in prayer every day. We will ask in faith and humility for God to bless each other with good health and energy, with divine wisdom for all decisions, and with self confidence to accomplish daily responsibilities.

4.   We will read and study the Bible together. We will select a daily devotion booklet that we can read together as a couple. We will

join a Bible Study Class or a Couples Bible Course for learning and sharing the inspired knowledge of God's Word.

5. We will seek the Holy Spirit with all our hearts, knowing He is the third person of the Holy Trinity. The Holy Spirit will guide us in all truth as Christ promised in John 14, and will keep us spiritually strong. We will research and study the Holy Spirit throughout the Bible knowing it is through God's Word that we can be renewed each day in the Spirit. We will discover how central He is in all of God's purposes for us to have an abundant and eternal life. We will seek to be <u>filled</u> with the Holy Spirit, as Ephesians 5:18 commands. We will endeavor to be <u>empowered</u> by the Holy Spirit, as Jesus instructs us in Acts 1:8. We will <u>live</u> in the Spirit as Galatians 5: 22-23 directs us.

Marriage is a sacred union given and blessed by God. Husbands and wives are to love each other as Christ loves the Church. He has given His very life for her existence. Christ is the Groom and the Church is His Bride. Marriage is to reflect the image of Divine Love through which Christ established the Church. The spiritual dimension of marriage is as essential to the oneness of a husband and wife as the heart is to the human body. Spiritual growth as individuals and as a couple is essential for the health and happiness of a Christian marriage. It assures a right relation with God. From this relationship will come peace, forgiveness, joy, and love that make this life-long journey the greatest venture a man and woman can ever experience.

Someone has wisely said, "When we fail to plan, we plan to fail." The four goals above constitute a plan for success in marriage. Each marriage begins as an uncharted course. Only God knows our future. But God guides us forward with goals to stay physically fit, mentally alive, financially secure, and spiritually strong. Committing ourselves in marriage to these goals can be the best investment we will ever make for the future happiness, health, and prosperity of our home.

CHAPTER NINE

WHAT SHALL WE WEAR?

Colossians 3:12-14, "*As God's chosen ones, holy and beloved, clothe your-selves with compassion, kindness, humility, meekness, and patience. Bear with one another and, if anyone has a complaint against another, forgive each other; just as the Lord has forgiven you, so you also must forgive. Above all clothe yourselves with love, which binds everything together in perfect harmony.*"

What to wear is a major decision in daily life, and this is particu-larly true for special occasions. The proper attire was the first thought that came to a man after reading a summons to appear before an IRS agent for an audit of his last year's income tax forms. He asked his accountant for advice as to what he should wear in order to make his best impression. He said, "Wear your shabbiest clothing. Let the IRS think you are poor as you can be."

Then he asked his lawyer the same question. Her answer was, "Don't let the IRS intimidate you. Wear your most elegant and expensive suit and tie."

Still confused as to what he should wear, the man went to his Rabbi and sought his advice. The Rabbi thought a minute and said, "Let me tell you a story. A woman who was planning her wedding and honey-moon asked her mother what she should wear on her wedding night. Her answer was, 'Wear a heavy, long, flannel nightgown that goes right up to your neck.' Dissatisfied with her mother's answer, she asked her closest friend the same question. She said, 'Wear a lacy see through nightgown with the sexiest underwear you can buy.'"

The man obviously frustrated with conflicting answers to his question said, "Rabbi, just what does that story have to do with my IRS appointment?"

The Rabbi replied with a twinkle in his eye, "My son, no matter what you wear, like the bride, you are going to be had."

Instead of being had on our wedding day, God makes us glad by providing us clothing we need every day in marriage. God's apparel, as described in Colossians 3: 12-14, is always a perfect fit. It makes us look our best in the eyes and hearts of others. This is why Proverbs 31: 30 says, "Charm is deceitful, and beauty is vain, but a woman who trusts in the Lord is to be praised." Christian husbands and wives who trust God for the spiritual garments needed for loving relationships become more attractive to each other than regular clothes and shoes could ever provide.

Can you imagine how wonderful it would be to live with your mate and best friend who dressed from God's wardrobe each day? I believe it would be like a honeymoon that never ended. The seven items God gives us to wear would radiate respect, consideration, joy, peace, and happiness wherever we are.

We are usually very good at wearing the appropriate clothing that fits the occasion or activity of our schedule. We know what the dress code is at the place of our employment. We carefully wear the items that are required by a sporting activity. A formal evening event guides our choice of clothing even to the smallest detail. Perhaps the one occasion that requires more thought and planning for the perfect attire is on our wedding day. We certainly want to look and feel our best when we stand before God, family, and friends to make our vows of marriage.

Since all of this is true, how much more important is our decision to be properly dressed after we are married? It is of first importance! The good news is that our loving God, in whom we place our trust, provides us with the clothing that will keep beauty and freshness in our marriage every day. Try on each of these seven items, and see if they don't fit perfectly. Ask your mate how you look and act when you are clothed with God's apparel.

THE FIRST IS COMPASSION. A Christian who is baptized into Jesus Christ becomes a new person. The old has passed away and behold the new has come. II Corinthians 5:18 says, "All this is from God, who reconciled us to Himself through Christ, and has given us the ministry of reconciliation." This new life puts off the old clothing of selfishness and puts on compassion. The Greek word for this first garment is "*Oiktirmos.*" It means that a Christian cares about you and your situation. A Christian has a new heart empowered by the Holy Spirit that seeks to act on your behalf with compassion. It is Christianity that brought civility to a harsh and ruthless world. Societies of the Greek and Roman empires were void of pity and compassion for those without money and power. Christianity introduced respect for all human life, even the unborn. More than any other religion or philosophy, Jesus Christ elevated women to their rightful place along with men as persons formed in the Image of God. About thirty years after the Resurrection of Jesus Christ, Paul's letter of Galatians 3:28, was teaching the world, "There is no longer Jew or Greek, there is no longer slave or free, there is no longer male and female; for all of you are one in Christ Jesus."

The compassion Christianity brought to the world also gave birth to hospitals that care for the sick, the aged, the mentally ill, the orphaned and unwanted of society. It established public education for the wealthy and the poor. It introduced humane treatment even for animals as a new standard of regarding all life as given of God.

Jesus illustrated God's gift of compassion by telling the parable of the Good Samaritan. The traveler from Samaria put aside his personal agenda to help a stranger who had been beaten, robbed, and left to die. He took him to a nearby Inn and paid for the man's care until he recovered. Jesus said we can all act for the good of others when the Holy Spirit changes our hearts and gives us compassion to wear as the first garment of our Christian clothing.

The very nature of compassion enables a husband and wife to live for each other's highest good. As you anticipate your mate's needs and offer help and encouragement, your mate is actively doing the same for you as circumstances permit. Compassion doesn't keep a score of who does the most for the other. It just cares enough to be there giving, sharing, praying, and providing what is helpful.

THE SECOND IS KINDNESS. I believe this garment is to be worn on the tongue. Some people pierce their tongues and wear precious metals in them. But God makes our tongues beautiful by adorning them with kindness. A husband who calls his wife from work on a day when he knows she is having a hard time and says, "I was thinking of you this morning and wanting you to know I stand with you no matter what happens." His words of kindness lift her spirits and lighten her burden.

In a similar way, a wife speaks with kindness to her husband one Sunday by saying, "I want to drive the Church youth van for you tonight.

You are exhausted, and I think you need to stay home and get some rest." Words of kindness become acts that strengthen the bond of marriage.

During the Christmas Season each year at our Church in Atlanta, we encourage our members to participate in "The Adopt A Family Program." Those who are willing receive the name and address of a family in the Atlanta area who are having financial difficulties. Information about their needs, clothing sizes, and ages of the children guide us in buying useful and fun items for Christmas. On a Saturday before Christmas Day, the gifts and items of food were delivered to each home on our Adopt A Family list. I remember one year when a group of us returned to the Church Fellowship Hall to share our experiences. A newly-married couple told about the wonderful time they had with a single mother of four children. Then the wife surprised all of us by saying, "I don't think I have ever loved my husband more than while visiting in the poverty of that home. When I heard him talk to that mother with such heartfelt kindness, I realized he was the most wonderful man I have ever known. I will always remember this Christmas because of this opportunity to help someone else."

It is really true as this young wife affirmed. Our respect for each other in marriage increases when we see and hear each other practice kindness. One of the best opportunities for kindness is while driving on the roads and highways of our towns and cities. It is so easy to be provoked by an aggressive or rude driver. The natural feeling is to react with hostility. But if we are wearing kindness we can show restraint. We can yield to the other driver and smile. The result of kindness makes the community a better place in which to live for everyone. Romans 12: 16-18 says, "Live in harmony with one another; do not be haughty...Do not repay anyone evil for evil, but take thought for what is noble in the sight of all. If it is possible, so far as it depends on you, live peaceably with all." In other words, just wear kindness wherever you go.

THE THIRD IS HUMILITY. This is a spiritual garment that indicates we know who we are. The word itself comes from the root word "humus." It refers to the earth from which we were created. The humble understand that God is the Creator and each person is the Created. The humble, therefore, honor and worship God and not themselves. They do not think of themselves more highly than they ought to think because they see all human life having equal value and dignity. Humility has nothing to do with self-depreciation or self-exaltation. It gives the balance between acknowledging God as Sovereign and Lord, and yourself as being created a very special person just like everyone else. Although there are many differences among people in personality, intelligence, and ability, we are equal in value by being uniquely designed by our Creator.

In marriage, humility is the antidote for arrogance and selfishness. A husband and wife with humility can confidently affirm they have been designed by the Most High God with divine value and potential. They therefore expect and encourage each other to achieve their very best in all their endeavors that make life and home fulfilling and harmonious. The different areas of authority, responsibility, and respect are accepted and appreciated in their marriage covenant. But because of their humility, neither seeks to dominate or take advantage of the other.

THE FOURTH IS MEEKNESS. The New Testament uses the Greek word *"prautes"* to communicate meekness. Jesus gave blessing to the meek as the ones who will inherit the earth (Matthew 5:5). The meek are not weak. They are self-actualizing persons who live within the restraints of what is right and true. They accept the authority of God over their lives and seek His Will above their own. The power of the Holy Spirit enables them to maintain self-control and to maximize their energy and ability toward accomplishing what is profitable for themselves and others.

In ancient times, wild horses were considered meek when they were harnessed and brought under the control of their riders. Yet the horses maintained their beauty, strength, and speed! They were just more productive when they lived within the restraints of their trainers than when they ran wild. They were regarded as being meek when they accepted the control and guidance of those who had authority over them.

So it is with us. God wants husbands and wives to wear the clothes of meekness in order to have self-control under His Authority. We live in an age of addictions. The opportunities to over indulge with food, alcohol, smoking, various kinds of drugs, pornography, greed, and corruption are ever present. Each of them reduces our abilities, wastes our time, compromises our character, and weakens our marriage. God invites us to be harnessed in meekness so we can choose and do what is right, what is productive, and what proves to be a blessing to our marriage, family, and friends.

Another expression for meekness is gentleness. Strength, power and influence can "take advantage" of others. But if we are gentle, we will treat others as we would like to be treated. Jesus was the most powerful person who ever lived. He had all authority in heaven and earth. He performed miracles that cured the sick, calmed the storm, raised the dead, and withstood all the temptations with which Satan attacked Him in the wilderness. Yet through it all, He was gentle. We too are to be gentle! Philippians 4:4 instructs us to "rejoice in the Lord always, letting all people know our gentleness, for the Lord is with us." When we are quick to anger and lose control of our strengths, we embarrass not only those near and dear to us, we also disappoint our Lord. He is with us at all times and He expects us to be gentle. We are to let all people know our gentleness, especially the one to whom we are married.

THE FIFTH IS PATIENCE. As we learned from the nature of God's Love, the very first quality of Agape is patience. The Greek word is *"markrothumia."* It refers to the Spirit of God within us that keeps hope alive. It refuses to give up when wrong attacks us and when hard times beset us. It enables us to endure disappointments and even criticisms without over-reacting. A man and woman in marriage bring so many differences to their relationship. It is exceedingly difficult to be "one" with someone who has different views, patterns of behavior, and preferences. Only patience can sustain a developing marriage so we can learn to compromise, adjust, and reason together. It takes time and unselfish effort. But love will provide this garment of patience to wear every day. The wife needs to see it on her husband, and the husband will benefit from his wife always wearing it in his presence.

The most frequent complaint Sandra has of me is waiting while I get ready to go somewhere. I don't like to be late, and it is very seldom that I am. But I don't like to be early for an appointment or an event. Sandra does. I can always think of one more thing to do before it is time to leave the house. I feel justified in living this way, but it is very frustrating to Sandra. It takes a lot of patience for her to wait for me to get ready. I do try to be considerate, but if it weren't for God's love that gives her patience, our marriage would be in big trouble!

THE SIXTH IS FORGIVENESS. One of the greatest stories the world has ever heard is the parable Jesus told about the prodigal son in the Gospel of Luke 15: 11-32. After the young boy insulted his father, left home, and wasted his inheritance in riotous living, he came to himself, arose from the mess he had made of his life, and returned to his father. When the father saw his boy coming down the road toward the farm house, he ran out to meet him. The father had not heard from him in a very long time. He feared his son was dead. With great joy, the father embraced his impoverished son who stood there in soiled and ragged clothes. The boy couldn't even look up into the eyes of his father. Burdened with shame and guilt he said, "Father, I have sinned against heaven and before you; I am no longer worthy to be called your son." But his dad said to the farm servants, "Quickly, bring out a robe - the best one - and put it on him...for this boy of mine was dead and has come to life; he was lost and has been found. Let us have a party and celebrate his homecoming!"

I believe the "Best Robe" the father had to put around the dirty shoulders of his son was the "White Robe of Forgiveness." This boy who had sinned in every way he could was made clean that day through the Grace of God. He was forgiven all of his iniquities and failures. He was restored as an honored son of the father. He wore the robe of forgiveness not only to the party that evening, but he wore it the rest of his life.

We too are like this young man to a greater or lesser extent. We have sinned and forfeited our right to be called a daughter or son of our Heavenly Father. But when we come to our true self, arise, and return to God with heartfelt confession of sin, we are forgiven. God places His "White Robe of Forgiveness" about our shoulders. God restores us as His own, not just in this life, but for all eternity. We wear this robe of forgiveness not only to claim our identity as a child of God, but also as a reminder that we are to forgive others as we have been forgiven.

As Christians redeemed by the Grace and Love of God, we enter marriage wearing this robe of forgiveness. We must not forget to put it on every day. We will need it to forgive one another. A wife and husband are not perfect in their attitude, speech, and behavior. Only Jesus Christ is Holy and without any wrong. We have many flaws. We are not to justify our wrong doing by claiming we are "only human". We are to strive to live according to God's Will and to be quick to apologize when we offend one another. When we confess our mistakes, we are asking for forgiveness – just as we want to be forgiven, we are "to forgive". At times it is very painful and only the Grace of God working in us can bring about true forgiveness. But forgive we must.

Several years ago, a husband from a six year marriage told me that he would never forgive his wife for what she did. He said he was so hurt and so angry, he could never love her again. I patiently heard him express his feelings. I hurt with him because I was his pastor. But when it was my turn to speak I said, "I agree with you." He was surprised. I said, "I know you cannot forgive her. I know you are angry and deeply hurt. I know you can never love her again. But this isn't just about you. It is about you and God."

I then asked him, "Didn't you receive the mercy and forgiveness of God when you became a Christian?" He said, "Yes of course." I asked him,

"Did you <u>deserve</u> to be restored by the Love and Grace of God?" He said, "No." I took a deep breath: "Yet, you were forgiven and you <u>accepted</u> God's Grace." I then opened my Bible that was on my desk to Romans 5. I asked him to listen to these words: "Since we are justified by faith, we have peace with God through our Lord Jesus Christ, through whom we have access to this Grace in which we stand...For while we were still weak, at the right time Christ died for the ungodly...God proves His Love for us in that while we still were sinners, Christ died for us. Much more surely then, now that we have been justified by His blood, will we be saved through Him from the wrath of God...Through our Lord Jesus Christ we have now received reconciliation."

I then said, "Your wife needs to be saved from your wrath. You are angry and rightfully so. You can't forgive her by yourself. But with God who forgave you and now gives you the power of His Grace, you can forgive her. Just as we have been forgiven, so we must forgive those who have wronged us. Unless you and I turn in our Robes of Forgiveness, we must do our best to forgive others. The Good News is that we don't have to do it alone. God is with us. He is the master of forgiveness. He enables us to do what otherwise we could not do."

After we talked a while longer and prayed together, he returned to his home. We had several other visits that seemed helpful to him. One day his wife came in to discuss the matter that had caused so much pain. She was remorseful for her mistakes and wanted her husband to forgive her. They each <u>experienced</u> reconciliation by God's Grace and moved forward in their marriage with honesty and forgiveness. After all this happened, I was delighted to see them become more active in the life of our congregation. This experience helped me learn more about the power of forgiveness. It was also an occasion for me to express joyful thanksgiving to God for His Grace as I saw evidence of new love sprouting in this couple's marriage. As best I know they are still together.

THE SEVENTH IS LOVE. The most important garment God gives us to wear in marriage is Love. Colossians 3: 14 says, "Above all, clothe yourselves with love, which binds everything together in perfect harmony." Love is the binding power that holds together everything that is important in marriage. Yes, we need to wear compassion, kindness, humility, meekness, patience, and forgiveness for marriage to have harmony. But love is the crown of all that we wear. This love is from God who Himself is Love. His love is greater than our human feelings of affection. It is more lasting than romantic love. It is more perfect than the desire to give ourselves to another. It is the means of forsaking all others and being faithful to our marriage partner for as long as life lasts.

This love enables a husband and wife to cherish each other, to honor each other, and to comfort and protect each other during the entire journey of marriage. I Corinthians 13: 13, says there are three essentials of life that everyone needs: faith, hope, and love. These three abide. But the greatest of these is LOVE. It is the one garment God provides that always shines and makes those within its light grow in joy, peace, and grace.

An unknown writer who knew the wonder of this kind of love wrote the following words:

"I love you, not only for what you are, but for what I am when I am with you.
I love you, not only for what you have made of yourself, but for what you are making of me.
I love you for the part of me that you bring out;
I love you for putting your hand into my heaped-up heart, and passing over all the foolish, weak things that you can't help dimly seeing there, and for drawing out into the light all the beautiful belongings that no one else had looked quite far enough to find.
I love you because you have done more than any creed could have done to make me good, and more than any fate could have done to make me happy.
You have done it without a touch, without a word, without a sign.
You have done it by being yourself.
Perhaps that is what being in love means after all."

CHAPTER TEN

G.R.O.W.ing SPIRITUALLY

Luke 11:1 *"Jesus was praying in a certain place, and after He had finished, one of His disciples said to Him, 'Lord, teach us to pray'."*

The disciples realized that prayer with God was the source of Jesus' power, purpose, and peace. Their lives in comparison to His were spiritually weak. His life was radiant, joyful, and in perfect harmony with God, Himself, others, and nature. They wanted to be able to pray as Jesus prayed. They boldly asked Him to teach them to pray. This is the only time in all of scripture that we hear the disciples ask Jesus to "teach them". Prayer was that <u>important</u> to them, for it was the very essence of Jesus' life.

Like Jesus' disciples, Christian couples sooner or later in their married life realize that communication with God is as important as their daily talking and sharing concerns with each other. They discover that prayer is the means of **growing** spiritually and knowing God's Will for their lives.

A young minister and his wife experienced these benefits of prayer during the first four years of their marriage. It was through prayer that God confirmed their love and led them to the decision to marry. It was prayer that guided them to a rural Church where they served effectively. The congregation grew with new members and activities that were a blessing to them and to the community. But the Church could only pro-vide a meager salary and a small housing allowance that barely paid for a one bedroom apartment. The situation was especially difficult for the young wife as she tried to manage with so little.

When a downtown Church learned of this young minister's abilities as a preacher and pastor, he was offered their Senior Minister position. A committee came and met with the couple to explain their terms of employment. The minister and his wife could hardly believe they were being offered a salary three times what they were making, plus a newly-renovated house that was five times larger than their present apartment. After the committee completed their visit, the couple embraced each other with laughter and excitement. The young minister then said, "We will have to spend much time in prayer seeking God's Will." She placed her hands on her hips and looking him squarely in the face said, "You spend all the time you want in prayer. As for me, I'm going upstairs and start packing."

Even though we all are sometimes guilty of by-passing God when we make important decisions (as this minister's wife seemed to do), we need to seek God's direction every day — as Jesus always did. God's Will is for our highest good! God alone sees the future. If, with all our hearts through faith in Jesus Christ, we will <u>seek</u> God's Will above our own, He will save us from mistakes and guide us toward what is best for us and others involved in our lives. Proverbs 3: 3-6 says, "Trust in the Lord with all your heart, and do not rely on your own insight. In all your ways acknowledge Him, and He will make straight your paths." Prayer is the life line that God provides for us to communicate with Him and to know His Will. It is our spiritual GPS that keeps us going in the right direction.

Christian marriage has two dimensions. The first is horizontal between a husband and wife who are committed to each other with full equality, affirmation, respect, encouragement, and love. The second is the vertical between God and a husband and wife. In this dimension, Jesus Christ restores the brokenness of humanity and overcomes the enmity between man and woman and God which sin caused. He restores the equality and oneness of man and woman that God intended from the beginning of creation.

Both dimensions need nurturing with good communication, mutual interest, and committed living. Scripture teaches us in the Christian Covenant of Marriage that a husband and wife are to love each other as Christ loves the Church, and gave Himself up for the Church's life (Ephesians 5: 21-33). We are also taught that we are to love God with all our heart, and with all our soul, and with all our strength, and with all our mind (Luke 10: 27). In loving God, we are to meditate upon His Holy Word in scripture, worship Him gladly, and "pray without ceasing", as I Thessalonians 5: 17 guides us to do. God wants to be with us and commune with us. He is always available. He awaits our coming to Him in prayer. Jesus is our example. He is our Teacher of prayer who says (Matthew 6: 9):

Pray then in this way: 'Our Father who art in Heaven
Hallowed be thy name
Thy Kingdom come
Thy will be done
On earth as it is in Heaven
Give us this day
Our daily bread
And forgive us our trespasses
As we forgive those who trespass against us
And lead us not in temptation
But deliver us from evil
For thine is the Kingdom
And the Power
And the Glory forever. Amen.

Jesus taught us: "So I say to you: ask...seek...knock..." (Luke 11: 9) and Jesus told his disciples: "...they should always pray" (Luke 18:1).

Husbands and wives who accept God as the central person in their Covenant of Christian Marriage benefit in so many ways as they pray individually and as a couple. The primary benefit of regular prayer is growing and maturing spiritually. The true nature of a person is more spiritual than physical! We are created in the very image of God who is, according to Jesus in John 4: 24, "Spirit and Truth." Hence, in order to develop to our full potential, spiritual growth is essential.

Over the years while doing marriage counseling, many couples have told me how difficult it is for them to pray on a regular basis. They often say that their minds wander when they do take time to talk with God. They lose concentration and begin thinking of other matters after they begin a conversation with their Heavenly Father. Early in my ministry, I too was guilty of this same thing. I became so busy I often did not take the time to pray. When I did, my prayers were brief and most frequently interrupted by other thoughts and concerns than the ones that I wanted to discuss with God.

The Holy Spirit convicted me of this problem, and I decided to learn to pray as Jesus my Lord asked me to do. I began a full study of the Bible to learn how people throughout the Old and New Testaments prayed. It was an amazing discovery for me! As I took notes and reflected on what I was learning, four words seem to be predominant in the prayer lives of people in scripture. I found that as these four words guided me in my morning prayers, I stayed more focused and experienced power and peace from God as I prayed.

The first letters of these words form the word G R O W. They represent:

G - GRATITUDE (Begin praying by expressing to God thanks for all the people, blessings, experiences, learning and travel opportunities, good health, etc. that have enriched your life.)

R - REPENTANCE (Confess to God the sins, mistakes, bad habits, negative attitudes, and selfish acts of your life that are contrary to God's Will. Believe God hears and forgives your sins.)

O - OTHERS (Name individuals for whom you want to pray. Be specific asking for God's blessings, healing, guidance, love, forgiveness, and mercy in their lives.)

W - WILL OF GOD (Present to God your needs, requests, decisions, hurts, and hopes. Ask God to help you know His Will and to surrender your will to what God knows is best for you.)

These four parts of sincere prayer are Biblically-based. They guide us in the exercise of our daily conversation with God. They are a great asset in helping us G.R.O.W. spiritually. They also cultivate our integrity as we seek to be true and honest persons.

We are never more honest than during an open discussion with God. We can't deceive our Creator. We can't in His Presence make ourselves seem any better or worse than we are. God already knows everything there is to know about us before we present our petitions and concerns to Him.

It is a wonderful experience to know we can be totally honest with God without feeling judged, rejected, or condemned. Honesty with God leads to receiving His Love, Mercy, Forgiveness, and Encouragement. The Gospel of John 3: 16-17 assures us that, "God so loved the world that He gave His Only Son that everyone who believes in Him may not perish, but may have eternal life. Indeed, God did not send the Son into the world to condemn the world, but in order that the world might be saved through Him."

After using the "G.R.O.W. Prayer" each morning for several months, I shared it with Sandra. I then asked if she would join me in taking turns praying to God the order of these four categories. She agreed, and we held hands as we prayed. She began praying out loud with words of GRATITUDE for the many blessings of her life. She then squeezed my hand, and I expressed to God the blessings for which I was thankful. I then squeezed her hand for her to REPENT. I love this part of hearing her confess her wrongs. She sometimes over does it when I repent by saying, "Amen" and "Yes Lord, it is so," and "Have mercy on him, Lord." I just ignore her, and we go on with our praying by mentioning OTHERS by name for whom we make intercession. We then take turns seeking the WILL of God in areas of our lives where we are struggling, confused, or uncertain as to what is right for us to do.

Through the years, we have experienced our "G.R.O.W. Prayer" to be very special in helping us grow spiritually. We try to keep each part specific and limited to about thirty seconds. Even though it takes only about ten minutes to pray together, it is amazing how much can be expressed in such a short amount of time. It is also surprising how different our prayers are for gratitude, repentance, other people, and God's Will to guide us in right living. We often will hold hands and pray this way while driving in the car. We turn the radio off, and experience the Presence of our Lord as we pray together. The driver, however, keeps his or her eyes open during the prayer. We pray this way when we take walks, or when we are together at special places like on the beach, in the mountains, or swinging in our patio swing. Since our engagement and throughout our marriage, we pray for each other and hold hands for a blessing before every meal we share. Yet, we can honestly say that no other experience has enriched our marriage more than overhearing each other talk with God by this way of praying.

When we pray together in this way, we experience three profound benefits. First, we find that we are more honest with our heartfelt thoughts, requests, and concerns than during any other conversation. Second, we experience an intimacy with each other that increases our shared love. When I hear Sandra express Gratitude to God for me and for what I mean to her, a joy wells up in my heart more pleasing than any other gift she could ever give me. Third, we experience true worship. As we talk to God and listen in silence for His spiritual guidance, we feel His Presence, His Power, and His Peace.

We have heard many couples through the years of our ministry say they have never prayed out loud together. They have prayed for each other, but never <u>with</u> each other. After we introduce this "G.R.O.W. Prayer" to them, we often receive reports of their having experiences similar to ours. They too find the orderliness of these four categories

helping them stay focused without a wandering mind. They also experience the honesty and new discovery of inner feelings that have not been
expressed before by overhearing their conversations with God. Also, and
most importantly, they tell us that they are growing spiritually as husband
and wife.

This kind of prayer brings to life the words of Philippians 4: 6-7: "Do
not worry about anything, but in everything by prayer and supplication
with thanksgiving let your requests be made known to God. And the
peace of God which surpasses all understanding, will keep your hearts
and your minds in Christ Jesus."

CHAPTER ELEVEN

THE JOY OF SEX

I Corinthians 7: 2b – 5a, *"Each man should have his own wife and each woman her own husband. The husband should give to his wife her conjugal rights, and likewise the wife to her husband. For the wife does not have authority over her own body, but the husband does; likewise the husband does not have authority over his own body, but the wife does. Do not deprive one another except perhaps by agreement for a set time, to devote yourselves to prayer, and then come together again."*

A husband was talking with a friend about their having a baby. He said, "We knew God made man and woman in His Image and said to them, 'Be fruitful and multiply.' Following God's instructions, we tried and tried for five years to have our first child. Finally, God blessed us with a healthy and wonderful son. We really didn't mind that it took us so long to conceive. We were having so much fun trying."

The gift of sex within the purity of marriage is a source of great joy. God's divine intentions for this treasure to man and woman is to unite them as one flesh enabling them to multiply and fill the earth (Genesis 1: 28). Paul explains in the scripture above: "Each man should have his own wife and each woman her own husband. The husband should give to his wife her conjugal rights, and likewise the wife to her husband." In the Covenant of Christian marriage, sex brings pleasure to both the husband and wife as unselfish love is expressed and shared. God's blessing is upon their sexual oneness, and there is no human experience of ecstasy so wonderful as this gift.

However, sex is often misrepresented in our world today. Much of the entertainment media presents sex as the most important experience in human life. The fashion world predominately highlights the seductive aspects of the human body to give the impression that sex determines the value and desirability of a man and woman. "Making love" is the term frequently used to imply that real and lasting love can be "made" through the act of sex.

All of these claims for sex are simply not so. Chip Ingram in his book, "Love, Sex, and Lasting Relationships" quotes a college basketball star who says, "I've been an idolater...worshipping me. When I began playing ball on the road, I got a real buzz from the crowd and I discovered I was attractive to ladies. There were times I had sex multiple times a day with different women. At first, it was the game outside the game; how often and with how many different coeds could I have sex with. I lost count of the number."

He continued his story by saying, "I went through about three years of this. Then I woke up one day and I was numb. I was a sexual burnout. My heart got dull, my brain wouldn't respond. I realized that a tiny piece torn from me was left with each of these women that I can never get back." He compared his selfish indulgence of sex to being a piece of cardboard. Sex with each woman was like two pieces of cardboard glued together and then torn apart. Something important from each life was left behind, never to be reclaimed again.

Chip Ingram concludes this true story with the young man's confession, "I got to where I didn't enjoy sex and I didn't like me. I was so far from God that I knew I was lost. I am now asking God little by little to heal me." The powerful Good News is that God will heal anyone who seeks forgiveness and a new beginning.

This story illustrates the ancient truth that "Evil is good misused." Sex is a wonderful and beautiful gift from God to be enjoyed within the fidelity of marriage. But when the ways of the world lure a person into misusing sex, and by it devaluing the worth and dignity of another man or woman, it becomes evil. Romans 6: 12-13 reminds us, "Therefore, do not let sin exercise dominion in your mortal bodies, to make you obey their passions. No longer present your members to sin as instruments of wickedness, but present yourselves to God as those who have been brought from death to life, and present your members to God as instruments of righteousness."

Instead of yielding to the world's false claims that sex alone determines the importance and desirability of a person, be steadfast in God's revealed truth. Throughout scripture, God makes clear that character, integrity, humility, unselfish living, and righteous behavior are more precious than gold and silver. Proverbs 31: 30 says, "Charm is deceitful and beauty is vain, but a woman who trusts the Lord is to be praised." Psalm 1: 1 teaches that, "Happy is the man who does not follow the advice of the wicked, but delights in the law of the Lord." Jesus in Matthew 6: 33, directs us to "Strive first for the kingdom of God and His righteousness, and all other things needed will be given to you." It is powerfully liberating to know that God approves *character* more than body shape, *integrity* more than popularity, and *genuineness* more than seduction. It is God whom we should seek to please and not the immoral standards of the world. As we measure our value and importance by God's righteous standards, we will not only have self confidence in who we truly are, but will be able to say with the Psalmist, "I will sing of your steadfast love, O Lord, forever; with my mouth I will proclaim your faithfulness to all generations. I declare that your steadfast love is established forever; your faithfulness is as firm as the heavens" (Psalm 89:1).

Therefore, with regard to human sexuality in marriage, there are five essential truths we need to know and believe. Since God created us and designed the male and female bodies to fit together, we can enjoy the intimacy of love and His Word, and not the ways of this fallen world. They will lead us to fulfillment in the bond of marriage.

First: sex is a good and divine gift from God.

Sex is not another entitlement provided by the government to a man and woman who have a legal marriage license. Sex is not a development by intelligent professors in a university lab. Sex is not the achievement of the evolutionary process. When God created man and woman in His Image, He presented them the gift of sex on the very day of their union in marriage. God declared the two of them one as only male and female bodies can join together as one flesh. God blessed them and said, "It was very good" (Genesis 1: 31). Sex is a positive word and a beautiful gift when we wait for the Giver to present it to us.

Somehow my faith as a Christian led me to this reality when I was sixteen years old. I remember with crystal clarity the afternoon I was sitting on a large boulder at the water's edge of a fast moving stream. My Scout troop was camping at Bolder Park which is near Atlanta, Georgia. I was alone and thinking about how great it would be if I had a girl friend. I began talking with God and asking for guidance. It was fun just thinking about who God had in mind for me, and when I would meet her. Immediately I began to realize God was preparing me for someone and preparing someone for me. My heart was filled with a peace and satisfaction that somewhere known only to God a young woman was growing and developing to become my future wife. Believing this to be true, I accepted the spiritual fact that I was already married at the age of sixteen. Sitting on that big rock, I was surprised to receive this revelation from God. I was delighted with the thought that "She is somewhere looking for me, and I will be searching for her." I resolved in that amazing experience to wait for God's good timing. I promised with God's enabling power to abstain from sexual intercourse until the day of marriage. I confess I had a number of girlfriends and enjoyed what we called "making out." But by God's Grace, I was able to keep my vow to God and to myself until September 23, 1967. I was twenty nine years old when God presented Sandra and me with His Divine Gift and enabled us to celebrate our oneness in marriage. Sandra tells a similar life story of saving her gift of sex for her future husband. We together were able to receive from God His beautiful gift, and then give to each other for the first time the secret of our sexual identities.

We share this personal information to illustrate the joy of sex when it is experienced as a gift. Everyone has a different story to tell. Some know the pain of having sex stolen from them. Others know the guilt of sex being misused. But everyone needs to know that God's intentions are for sex to be a gift. It begins with His great gift to man and woman, and its full joy is realized when a husband and wife lovingly give this gift to each other.

Selfish demands for sex shatter the gift. True love increases the joy of giving sex to affirm the one you adore, and to satisfy their physical needs with pleasure. The important element is the intent within the heart of each partner to please the other. When concern for the other's fulfillment pervades sexual exchange, then true joy abounds for both.

Second: sex outside the Covenant of Marriage is wrong and guilt producing.

The misuse of sex diminishes the joy God's gift intends to provide. When marriage begins, a husband and wife promise to forsake all others and be faithful to each other as long as life lasts. Since there is no one else to fulfill sexual desires, a husband and wife give each other authority over their own bodies (I Corinthians 7:4). Sensitivity, generosity, and unselfish caring are, therefore, crucial for each to give and receive sex. When the conjugal rights are given to each other, marriage is fulfilled. The need to seek satisfaction outside the bond of marriage is removed.

God's Word is very precise and clear about this matter. The Seventh Commandment instructs us not to commit adultery (Exodus 20:14). Proverbs 6:23 – 25 teaches, "The Commandment is a lamp and the teaching a light, and the reproofs of discipline are the way of life to preserve you from the wife of another, from the smooth tongue of the adulteress. Do not desire her beauty in your heart, and do not let her capture you with her eyelashes; for a prostitute's fee is only a loaf of bread, but the wife of another stalks a man's very life." Hebrews 13:4 highlights the importance of faithfulness by declaring, "Let marriage be held in honor by all, and let the marriage bed be kept undefiled; for God will judge people who are immoral and those who commit adultery."

Sex, when experienced as God intends, brings great joy. When sex is misused, devastating guilt results. After King David committed adultery with Bathsheba (II Samuel 11), he later confessed in Psalm 51:3, "For I know my transgressions and my sin is ever before me. Against you, O God, and you alone, have I sinned, and done what is evil in your sight." The short term pleasures from infidelity are never worth the price paid by the torment of guilt.

A husband or wife who carries the burden of guilt from sexual sins will find release in the sinner's prayer. David prayed it by saying, "Have mercy on me, O God, according to your steadfast love; according to your abundant mercy blot out my transgressions. Wash me thoroughly from my iniquity, and cleanse me from my sin" (Psalm 51: 1-2). Jesus Christ with love and power takes upon Himself our iniquities. I John 1: 7-9 assures us, "The blood of Jesus, God's Son, cleanses us from all sin. If we say that we have no sin, we deceive ourselves, and the truth is not in us. If we confess our sins, He who is faithful and just will forgive us our sins and cleanse us from all unrighteousness."

Only in this way can the barriers of guilt be removed and the joy of sex in marriage be fully realized. A minister of the gospel of Jesus Christ or a Christian counselor can be of assistance in helping a husband or wife work through the process of receiving God's forgiveness. Then, by God's Grace, forgiveness of self can renew one's spirit to fully love and be loved.

Third: sex is greater and more important than just a physical act of pleasure.

A psychologist at a medical conference presented a recent study about the frequency of sexual relationships in marriage. He reported that they averaged about twice a week. He then developed the point that if the act of sex takes about thirty minutes twice a week, that is one hour. Fifty two hours a year equals about one weekend. He concluded by saying that as much as sex is enjoyed in marriage, fifty two hours each year will not establish happiness in marriage. Greater effort and much more time than is spent on sex are needed to maintain a functioning companionship. The main focus for a husband and wife should be placed on the factors that develop a genuine love relationship which contributes to their mutual happiness.

Some of these factors are:

Practice thoughtful acts of consideration every day,

1) Show sincere interest in the feelings, concerns, and needs of each other
2) Develop the skills of listening and responding to each other with understanding
3) Cultivate the art of verbal communication along with personal notes and e-mails
4) Plan together the weekly schedule
5) Agree to share household responsibilities
6) Grow together spiritually through prayer, devotional reading and Bible study
7) Honor God in regular worship with a community of Christian faith.

When these priorities are established with harmony and affirmation for each other, the times of sex become a celebration of marital love and not a substitute for it. Weekly sex will be a blessing to a husband and wife and not just a duty. The benefits of this kind of sex, according to medical research, include better sleep at nights, decrease in heart attacks, reduction of stress and frustration, increase in the longevity of life, and women realize improvements in their menstrual patterns that lead to better fertility.

Therefore, sex understood as God's gift that a husband and wife share with each other because of their authentic love proves to be more valuable than just a physical act. Sex is God's invitation to experience the wonder of personhood, heart, and soul with another who is passionately committed to your highest good for as long as you live. In so doing, a husband and wife experience not only their love for each other, but also the greatness of God whose "Steadfast Love endures forever, and Faithfulness is a blessing to all generations" (Psalm 100: 5).

Fourth: sex for a husband and wife requires knowing and understanding each other.

The joy of sexual pleasure as God intends it is far more than the stimulation of body parts. It is the engagement of two whole persons who seek to love, honor, and cherish each other. Genitals therefore, are not the only, nor even the most important, organs that deliver sexual fulfillment. It doesn't take a scientist in sexual studies to verify that the "organ between our ears guides sexual pleasure more than the organ between our thighs." Sexually active adults realize that attitudes, emotions, and feelings are as essential to the joy of sex as genital interaction.

This is why the Holy Bible, which is God's instruction manual for a happy marriage, speaks of sexual intimacy as "knowing." For example, Genesis 4:1 says, "Now the man knew his wife Eve, and she conceived and bore Cain," and in verse 17, "Cain knew his wife, and she conceived and bore Enoch." Not knowing refers to young women who are virgins as in Numbers 31:18, "All the young girls who have not known a man by sleeping with him..." Sexual intimacy implies, according to the One who made us, an understanding of the whole person — body, mind, heart, and soul. It is to "know and to be known" in the most personal way possible.

Therefore, it is reasonable to conclude from God's Word that the joy of sex develops as a husband and wife get "to know" each other in the deepest aspects of their personalities. Satisfying sex doesn't just happen. It is a process of learning and sharing mutual respect for the different attitudes, needs, desires, and feelings that a man and woman have about sex. The guessing game will not accomplish this. Even though we like to be surprised by the other "knowing" what we want, greater effort is required. A husband and wife need to teach each other what arouses their sexual feelings and even fantasies. They need to tell and sometimes show each other when, where, and how they like to be touched. This informs love with "knowing" so every effort can be made to please the other. The pattern of a wife submitting to her husband as unto the Lord, and a husband loving his wife as he loves his own body just as Christ loves the Church(Ephesians 5:21 – 33), leads to the lifelong joy of sexual satisfaction.

One of the most helpful ways for a husband and wife "to know each other" is to identify their particular way of being loved and appreciated. Gary Chapman in his popular book, "The Five Love Languages", believes each husband and wife has a primary preference for being loved. It is the signal that he or she is truly cherished and valued. He lists these five love motivators as the following:

1) Encouraging words: verbally expressing appreciation, affirmation, approval, and love.
2) Quality time: making togetherness a priority each day without distractions.
3) Gift giving: thoughtful gifts for special occasions and appropriate times to say, "I love you."
4) Acts of service: anticipating your mate's needs and doing thoughtful things that really help.
5) Physical touch: hugs and kisses, holding hands, touching in public to say I'm here and I care.

Although, each of us may enjoy all five of the languages of love, there is one in particular that reaches our heart most directly. It is essential for a husband and wife to know which one is most motivating to each of them. By acting on this knowledge, the success of giving and receiving love will be more frequent than guessing what pleases the other. Just because you most appreciate gifts or touch doesn't mean the other does. You need "to know" each other's love language, and do your best to speak it. The full "Joy of Sex" as God intends it will be yours to enjoy.

Fifth: sex with thanksgiving mirrors the Image of God as two become one flesh.

Thanksgiving is the natural response of a husband and wife when sex is experienced as the intimate expression of their genuine love for each other. Who is the ultimate recipient of our thanksgiving? God is. He is the One who designed the mystery and wonder of sex. God is the One who presents sex as a sacred gift to a married couple. In the sharing of this gift, the Image of God is spiritually stamped in the marital union.

This became surprisingly true for me when Sandra and I married in 1963. As Christian teenagers long before we ever met, she and I decided by God's Grace and Power to reserve sexual intercourse for the one we someday would marry. When we began our journey of marriage, it was an extraordinary experience when we gave ourselves to each other. There was no greater gift we could have given to each other to express our love and vows of marriage than our virginity. The surprising emotion that over-whelmed me each time we shared this gift was thanksgiving. It seemed strange to me that out of the joy of having sex with my wife, a deep sense of praise and thanksgiving to God flowed from my heart. It was a natural, effortless, and unplanned response. Even before I ever read and consid-ered the theological implications of marriage being a sacred gift, a gen-uine sense of God's Presence increased my joy of sex.

Through the years as I matured in marriage the reason for these feel-ings of thanksgiving became obvious to me. Since "Agape" is the love God gives us to share in marriage, the experience of this love connects us with the God of our being. I John 4: 16 makes this wonderfully clear. He declares, "God is love and those who abide in love abide in God, and God abides in them." Anyone in the Covenant of Christian Marriage who gives and shares "Agape" in the intimacy of sex will experience the Spiritual Presence of God. Feelings of gratitude will come naturally, and worship and praise of God will freely flow from the heart. I can truthfully say that the times I feel the most joyful oneness with Sandra and God are the times of sexual fulfillment.

Many couples do not save the gift of their virginity for the one they marry. Everyone has their own stories to tell about the pleasant and unpleasant times of sexual intimacy. But regardless of one's circumstances and previous situations, a man or woman who accepts God's redeeming love and merciful forgiveness can celebrate the newness of life in the Covenant of Marriage. God makes clear in The Book of Revelation 21: 5b – 6b, "See I am making all things new... for these words are trustworthy and true... I am the Alpha and the Omega, the beginning and the end." Therefore, be assured that God can take our past and give to each of us through faith in Jesus Christ a new beginning! The old passes away, and the new becomes our present with thanksgiving. As a matter of fact, Jesus our Lord says in Luke 7: 47, "One who has been forgiven much is able to love much." In this way, a husband and wife will discover the wonder of love and the joy of sex as sacred gifts from God that move them to wor-ship and thanksgiving.

Dietrich Bonhoeffer wrote about this essence of Christian marriage in a masterful sermon named, "A Wedding Sermon From Prison." He was a Christian pastor who courageously renounced Adolf Hitler and his evil

Third Reich by calling Germany to repent and return to the God of Love, Truth, and Justice. Before his tragic execution in a German prison during World War II, he spoke of Christian marriage in the following way:

"Marriage is more than your love for each other. It has a higher dignity and power, for it is God's holy ordinance, through which He wills to perpetuate the human race until the end of time. In your love, you see only your two selves in the world, but in marriage you are a link in the chain of the generations, which God causes to come and to pass away to His Glory, and calls into His Kingdom. In your love, you see only the heaven of your own happiness, but in marriage you are placed at a post of responsibility towards the world and mankind. Your love is your own private possession, but marriage is more than something personal It is a status, an office... As high as God is above man, so high are the sanctity, the rights, and the promise of marriage above the sanctity, the rights, and the promise of love. It is not your love that sustains the marriage, but from now on, the marriage that sustains your love."

This I believe is the marriage God first gave to Adam and Eve, and the marriage He wills for each husband and wife to enjoy. It is a sacred treasure to be shared in love, for love, and with love because God is Love. The Image of God is reflected in this love that unites as one flesh a husband and wife. The sex they share not only brings them great joy, it also ushers them into a spiritual sanctuary of thanksgiving for God's generosity. There is no high a man and woman can experience as high as this high of love's intimacy given by the One who is The Most High.

CHAPTER TWELVE

THE "I" IN MARRIAGE

Ephesians 4: 1-6, *"I beg you to lead a life worthy of the calling to which you have been called, with all humility and gentleness, with patience, bearing with one another in love, making every effort to maintain the unity of the Spirit in the bond of peace. There is one body and one Spirit, just as you were called to the one hope of your calling, one Lord, one faith, one baptism, one God and Father of all, who is above all and through all and in all."*

Paul is stressing the importance of unity in this scripture from Ephesians. It is helpful because unity is the heart of marriage. A husband and wife join together their lives, faith, hopes, and values. The essence and future of their marriage depends upon the love and health of their unity. This is a great challenge for all married couples because of the many innate differences a man and woman bring to their relationship.

Highlighting these differences was a debate over the gender of computers. An equal number of men and women were given the task to determine if the nature of a computer was male or female. After much discussion the women announced that computers had to be male because of the following facts:

1. In order to get their attention, you have to "turn them on."
2. Computers have lots of data, but they are still clueless.
3. They are supposed to solve problems, but most of the time they are the problem.

4. After you commit to a particular computer, you realize that if you had waited just a little longer, you could have chosen a better model.

The group of men came to a different conclusion. Because of the following facts, they determined that the gender of computers had to be female:

1. No one but their creator understands their logic, temperament, and mood swings.
2. Computers can communicate and network among themselves, but their language is unknown to men.
3. Computers will store the smallest mistakes in their long term memory and retrieve them at the most inappropriate time.
4. After you commit to a particular computer, half your salary is then spent on buying all the accessories required to enhance its performance.

Stories like this make us laugh, but <u>differences</u> can either divide us or enrich us! God, who is the author of differences, wants the latter for us. God created man and woman uniquely different, and He gave them marriage to unite them as husband and wife. There is one thing that unites us or divides us. It is the "I."

The "I" is the individual self or the ego, as psychologists would identify it. The position the "I" takes makes all the difference in every relationship. The "I" can function with love and unselfishness and contribute to a relationship that is UNITED. The "I" can also function with uncompromising self-determination and cause a relationship to become UNTIED. It all depends upon a person's decision as to where his or her "I" will be placed.

Many times during my years of ministry of counseling married couples who were experiencing problems and difficulties, the one issue that seemed to cause most of their troubles were their differences. As each explained their point of view, it was clear that they were telling the truth. Each could make a compelling case that they were in the right, and the other was just being "stubborn". As I tried to understand both the husband's and wife's position, I learned from experience to ask a disarming question. It was, "Which is more important to each of you: To be right, or to be married?" I explained that they would always have differences. There is no way to avoid this reality. But for the sake of UNITY, I asked,

"Can you reposition your 'I' with love and tolerance so you can *appreciate* your differences without allowing them to divide you?"

Usually my question to troubled couples was followed by their question to me, "Just how do we learn to be UNITED instead of UNTIED?" My answer was simple. "God is responsible for the basic differences in our lives. God can, therefore, teach us how to live with our unique qualities while at the same time appreciating each other's differences. Our Triune God exists as One even though He is God The Father, God The Son, and God The Holy Spirit. The Unity of God is the means of our Unity in marriage. The loyalty of a husband and wife to the Covenant of their relationship reflects their loyalty to the Covenant they have with God."

God's revelation in Ephesians 4, which began this chapter, teaches us the seven spiritual realities that constitute and maintain the dynamic UNITY we need and want in marriage. They are:

1) One Body - The Church is the Body of Christ, advancing the Kingdom of God on earth.
2) One Spirit -The Holy Spirit fills us with joy, truth, and power to have the Unity of Love.
3) One Hope - The assurance that God is with us through faith in Christ, and hope guides us.
4) One Lord - Jesus Christ is Lord, and "In Him all things hold together" (Colossians 1:17).
5) One Faith - We are justified by faith and made one with God for eternal salvation.
6) One Baptism – All who are baptized into Christ are baptized into His death and resurrection.
7) One Father – God, our Heavenly Father, makes us one with Himself through Jesus Christ.

This unity with God makes possible our UNITY in Christian marriage. God the Holy Spirit enables us to keep the "I" in marriage where it belongs. We are able to avoid becoming UNTIED because God the Son enables us to be "humble, gentle, patient, and bearing with one another in love" (Ephesians 4:2). We then are empowered by God The Father to "make every effort to maintain the unity of the Spirit in the bond of peace" (Ephesians 4:3).

I have therefore, always encouraged couples during premarital counseling sessions to seek righteous counsel (as Proverbs 19:20 advises) when they encounter differences that try to pull them apart. God's truth and guidance from His Holy Bible opens a way when there doesn't seem to be a way. God can smooth the rough places in the journey of marriage. Proverbs 3: 5-6 are powerful and true words that offer Godly advice, "Trust in the Lord with all your heart, and do not rely on your own insight. In all your ways acknowledge Him, and He will make straight your paths" (Proverbs 3: 5-6).

There are many counselors who do not give righteous counsel. Their religion is personal happiness and individual satisfaction. Often when couples come to them for advice, they tell them, "If you aren't happy, just leave." Dr. Frank Pittman, a prominent psychiatrist in Atlanta, Georgia, identifies these counselors as "therapists who don't believe in marriage." He says, "They believe in marriage euthanasia...that their job is to put marriages to sleep when difficult problems develop."

Dr. Michele Weiner-Davis of Woodstock, Illinois, disagrees with therapists who advocate this philosophy. She has written a book from her years of providing psychiatric services that is entitled "Divorce Busting." She says many counselors focus too much on the pain and hopelessness a couple feels at the moment, instead of on the value of the investments they have placed in their marriage. She is convinced that most marriages are worth saving simply because most problems are solvable. Issues such as poor communication, boredom, nagging, lack of affection, and basic differences, she says, are the underlying *causes* of most marital problems. Most couples willing to learn from Godly counsel and to take positive steps to restore the unity of their marriage can overcome their troublesome differences.

She gives an example of helping one couple move the "I" from UNTIED to UNITED by agreeing not to discuss the details of their work each evening when they come together. The wife would ask her husband, "How was your day at the office?" Typically, he would gripe about his job and the work conditions of the office. She then would offer advice because she was very happy and successful in her career. This inevitably would infuriate him, and their evening would be ruined again. After the wife learned not to "deal with the differences" of their job situations, the arguments stopped. They began to have more fun together. They restored the unity of their marriage just by having more positive attitudes and encouraging communication. Dr. Weiner-Davis says such techniques as this one work with most marriages when couples are willing to follow righteous counsel based on understanding, patience, and unselfish love.

The rush to divorce should not be an option for couples who began their marriage in Covenant with God. God's Will for married couples is faithfulness and unity. His Word in Malachi 3: 14-16 says, "The Lord was a witness between you and the wife of your youth, to whom you have been faithless, though she is your companion and your wife by covenant. Did not one God make her? Both flesh and spirit are His. And what does the one God desire? Godly offspring. So look to yourselves, and do not let anyone be faithless to the wife of his youth. For I HATE DIVORCE, says the Lord."

Jesus confirmed this in a conversation with some Pharisees. In Mark 10: 1-9, they asked Him, "Is it lawful for a man to divorce his wife?" He answered them, "What did Moses command you?" They said, "Moses allowed a man to write a certificate of dismissal and to divorce her." But Jesus said to them, "Because of your hardness of heart he wrote this commandment for you. But from the beginning of creation, 'God made them male and female.' For this reason a man shall leave his father and mother and be joined to his wife, and the two shall become one flesh.' So they are no longer two, but one flesh. Therefore what God has joined together, let no one separate."

Except in rare occasions, divorce is not the answer. Yet, the forces of darkness in this world continue to lure people away from God's Will and make divorce an easy escape from present problems. California was the first state in America to pass the "No-fault Reforms" in 1969, which eliminated fault from divorce grounds and financial settlements. This virtually removed all protections of marriage as a sacred covenant. Other states quickly followed California's decision, and by 1985, all 50 states had adopted "No-fault Divorce." Once fault was removed, the frequency of divorce increased rapidly. This opened the way for a spouse to unilaterally file for divorce without the consent of their partner in marriage. Divorce now can be automatically granted to anyone who claims their marriage is "irretrievably broken". The spouse who seeks <u>solutions</u> to marital problems instead of divorce is powerless to prevent dissolution.

Unfortunately for God's Institution of marriage, the vows of marriage in America have become less binding than the average business contract. These "No-fault Divorce" laws now protect the defaulting party at the <u>expense</u> of his or her partner in marriage and the children their marriage has produced. "Focus on the Family", a Christian Ministry located in Colorado Springs, Colorado, has compiled the data from numerous studies on the consequences of divorce. It convincingly shows that divorce has huge public costs in billions of dollars for loss of tax income, child support enforcement, Medicaid, Assistance to Needy Families, food stamps, public housing, drug and alcohol related problems, increased expenses for correctional facilities, unwed childbearing, school delinquency problems, and a host of other social maladies that weaken local communities.

Studies also report that children with divorced parents, compared to children in stable homes with married mothers and fathers, are more likely to have poorer living conditions, more behavior problems, less educational attainment, more depression, and greater use of illegal drugs. Clearly, America's "No-Fault Divorce" policies have weakened God's plan for marriage with disastrous fiscal, societal, and individual consequences. Every effort should be given to assist and encourage persons affected by divorce. They do not need criticism and judgment. They need compassion and hope. Even greater efforts need to be given couples who enter marriage: helping them be <u>faithful</u> to their promises and committed to their marriage for as long as they live.

As a happily married man for over forty years, I can confidently and gratefully report that God's plan for marriage leads to success. Millions of other couples will also confirm this to be true. The devastation of divorce should be avoided. Embracing faithfulness, patience, and love should be the goals of every married couple. It is basically a matter of where the husband and wife will place the "I." We can enjoy and benefit from pursuing the UNITY of marriage, or by moving the "I" in the wrong direction, we will experience the hurt and misery of being UNTIED.

An unknown author wrote one of my favorite poems. These words affirm it is best to keep the "I" where God wants it to be. Glen Campbell used these words in a song to declare there should be a "little less of me" and a lot more "love for others." Read it and see if you don't agree:

"Let me be a little kinder; Let me be a little blinder
to the faults of those about me;
Let me praise a little more;
Let me be, when I am weary,
just a little bit more cheery;
Let me serve a little better those that I am striving for.
Let me be a little braver
when temptation bids me waver;
Let me strive a little harder to be all that I should be;
Let me be a little meeker with
the brother that is weaker;
Let me think more of my neighbor
and a little less of me."

CHAPTER THIRTEEN

THE FIVE "T's" OF MARRIAGE

Jeremiah 33: 10-11, *"There shall once more be heard the voice of mirth and the voice of gladness, the voice of the bridegroom and the voice of the bride, the voices of those who sing, as they bring thank offerings to the house of the Lord:*

Give thanks to the Lord of hosts, for the Lord is good,
For His steadfast love endures forever!"

A group of fourteen men came to our home in Mid-Town Atlanta every Friday for sixteen years. We met at 7:30 A.M. to share our Christian faith, study various books of the Bible, and spend some time together in prayer. I assumed their motivation to come every week was for spiritual growth. As time went on, I realized that their eager participation was prompted more by the full breakfast I prepared for them. Some of these highly successful businessmen and entrepreneurs admitted that it was the best breakfast (with hot biscuits) they got all week.

One Friday morning during our study on Christian marriage, I asked the group of men if they remembered the Five "T's" of marriage that I taught several years before. Their faces brightened, and one by one the men called out topics of marriage that begin with a "T." I was shocked when I heard them say:

1. Take out the Trash
2. Train your woman to be a good wife
3. Temper and Tantrums
4. Temptations
5. Trials and Tribulations

Obviously my previous teachings about having a happy marriage were in vain!

The intent behind my question to those men was to have a discussion about the verses from the Book of Jeremiah which began this chapter. I wanted to know what they thought it would take to keep the sound of "mirth and gladness" in their marriages! Jeremiah speaks of the voice of the bridegroom and the voice of the bride singing. We all would like to hear these sounds of happiness in our homes every day. I then asked the group, "What can a husband and wife do to promote a joyful and healthy relationship that would cause their hearts to want to sing?"

I suggested that activating the "Five T's of Marriage" is the best way I know to attain this goal. These "T's" are easy to remember. Through the centuries, couples have proven them effective for increasing satisfaction in their marriages. When practiced each day, the five "T's" act like catalysts to promote security, belonging, and gladness in the hearts of husbands and wives.

THE FIRST "T" IS TRUST

Trust is the confidence love needs to survive. It is the bedrock of any marriage. All relationships between a man and woman begin superficially. The process of getting acquainted takes time. Before intimacy occurs, a level of trust needs to be verified. Before a lasting commitment is made, mutual confidence in each other's trustworthiness should be established. You do yourself a great favor by opting out during the period of courtship if a pattern of dishonesty is evident. However, once trust is assured, true love can develop. Your innermost thoughts, feelings, and hopes can be shared with confidence. Your relationship matures on the foundation of unconditional trust. Marriage then can become a reality and not just a fantasy with the hope that things will get better.

Once trust is confirmed and the vows of marriage are declared, a husband and wife should treasure the gift of trust more than their rings of silver, gold, and diamonds. Just as you would agonize over the loss of your wedding ring, the loss of trust is a greater tragedy. Count it a priority in your daily living as husband or wife, and never lose it. Trust should be confirmed with honesty about small issues as well as major decisions. It is especially true regarding financial matters. Don't try to keep secrets about your spending habits. It is healthy to have regular conversations about income, spending, credit, and savings. Endeavor to be transparent about all money issues.

This is also true about keeping your word. When you promise to do something, do your best to deliver what is expected. Clarify your expectations with honest conversation to avoid disappointments. When you cannot meet an expectation your mate has of you, discuss it until an acceptable agreement is achieved. Trust is nurtured when the husband and wife take the initiative to share information, discuss schedules, and include the other in making decisions for the happiness of their home.

Another aspect of trust is confidentiality. As best friends a husband and wife share the most personal and intimate matters of their lives. This is a sacred trust. There needs to be conscious effort to protect each other's privacy and dignity. Even the smallest issues should not be shared with family members, friends, and colleagues at work without permission. A husband and wife should ask each other if it is OK to tell a mother, father, brother, sister, or friend about a personal matter. Keep trust alive and strong.

THE SECOND "T" IS TIME

Someone has truthfully said, "Time is the most valuable thing we ever spend." We can give special and thoughtful gifts to our mate in marriage, but when all is said and done, the time that we freely give for the enjoyment of being together is the gift most treasured. I have conducted many funerals during my active ministry. I have never heard anyone say of the deceased, "His or her greatest regret was not having spent more time at work." Instead, if they had life to live over again, they would spend more time with their family.

Marriage, therefore, should begin with prioritizing time. When there is a chronic time deficit for each other, marriage suffers. Careers, work, hobbies, children, Church, and personal activities compete for our time every day. There are many things we have to do. But the commitment to invest loving and focused time with each other is vital to a healthy and happy marriage. When husbands and wives have been apart because of daily work, some couples after they get home try to stay within five feet of each other for the first ten minutes. They share this time with affection and genuine interest in each other's feelings from the activities of the day. They try to avoid distractions and keep frequent eye contact with each other to indicate they are really listening. This gift of time sets the mood and atmosphere for the entire evening.

Do not be deceived by the excuse that it is the quality of time that counts and not the quantity. Both are important and appreciated.

Consider a seven course meal. Would you prefer such a meal with high quality taste that provided only a bite of each serving, or would you like to have both; a full serving with excellent taste? Consider another example of quality versus quantity. Would you like to have a sip of the finest wine money could buy, or would you rather enjoy a full glass of wine from a good vintage? Any reasonable person would say they want both good quality and sufficient quantity. So it is with our partner in marriage. We need and want both when it regards time with our lover and best friend.

Even after marriage has become a way of life, planning a date with each other several times a month is a wonderful gift. It confirms how valuable a husband and wife are to each other. Sandra and I endeavored to do this each Monday evening during the early years of our ministry. After our two daughters were born, we continued having a night out just for us. We knew that a happy marriage set the stage for a happy family. Children learn from their parents. When they see mother and father in love with each other and enjoying time together, this prepares them for their future marriages.

Sometimes it is necessary for a husband or wife to work overtime. There are also times when work is brought home to be completed during the evening. In order for these activities to be accepted, consideration for your mate with a clear explanation needs to be given. After the work is done, every effort should be made to give each other time to catch up with feelings, issues, and concerns.

Television and computer activities can prevent couples from spending time together. Attitudes and preferences regarding these "time grabbers" need to be discussed to reach mutual and satisfying agreements. Television in the bedroom most often proves to be an intruder when a husband or wife wants undivided attention. The bedroom is the place of intimacy, and it is best to keep the computer and TV in another room. Always remember time is our most valuable asset. How we use it communicates loud and clear our priorities. Make sure time is generously given to the love of your life.

THE THIRD "T" IS TALK

Marriage is a lifelong conversation between a man and woman who by God's Grace are committed to each other in the oneness of love. Talk is, therefore, essential for marriage to be healthy and happy. It is also a skill that requires a lot of practice, learning, and listening.

Some couples have great difficulty developing this important skill. One husband responded to the subject of talking by admitting, "I haven't talked with my wife in years. I thought it would be rude of me to interrupt her." A wife said to her husband reclined in his chair before the TV, "I have been talking to you for twenty minutes, and you haven't made a sound in response. I know you are in there. I can see your eye balls." Betty came into the kitchen one afternoon and noticed her husband Fred hunting flies with a fly swatter. "Have you hit any flies?" she asked. "Yep," Fred said. "I got four male flies and three females." Intrigued by his answer, she asked, "How the heck can you tell which is which?" "Easy," he answered. "I got the four males on the beer can, and the three females on the telephone."

These stories reflect the humor of husbands and wives trying to communicate, but they don't reveal the importance and value of meaningful dialogue that marriage requires. Psychologists and counselors from many different backgrounds agree on at least one thing; good communication between husbands and wives account for most of their marital stability and happiness. They also agree that poor communication tops the causes for discord and dissatisfaction in marriage. There are certain principles that promote "good talk" which help couples succeed in sharing life together.

The first is understanding the natural differences in the way a man and woman think and communicate. Men like report talk. This is bottom line information that gets to the facts in order to identify appropriate actions that lead to solutions. Women usually want rapport talk. This is connecting with feelings, emotions, and harmony in the relationship. In general men want to give advice, fix the problem, and move on to something else. Women want a discussion, assurance she is being taken seriously, understanding of her feelings, and appreciation for what she is trying to do. When husbands and wives understand and accept these basic differences, they are better equipped to make the necessary adjustments in their conversations with each other. A husband learns his wife sometimes just wants him to listen with empathy without giving advice and jumping to a solution. A wife learns her husband has feelings too, and often needs affirmation for what he accomplishes. In spite of all the differences, it is good for a man to be a man and for a woman to be a woman while learning to talk with mutual respect.

The second principle for marital talk is intentionality. It is important for a husband and wife to agree on a given time to talk often if not every day. During this "talk time" all distractions are put on hold. Body language and eye contact are focused for maximum listening and dialogue.

Permission is given for each to share honest feelings no matter what they are. The rules of engagement include no criticisms, interruptions, turning away, exaggerations, or "You Messages" that blame the other. Instead, "I Messages" are given to indicate how you feel, what you want, how you see certain issues, and what your hopes and hurts are. Occasionally this "talk time" should be used to exchange the ten characteristics you like most about each other, as well as the ten traits you dislike the most. When this is done just for the enjoyment of having a reality check, it is amazing how much fun it can be, and how much you can learn about each other.

The third principle in talking with your mate is having a positive attitude. Attitude is a choice, and love should always lead in the direction of what is good, affirming, and productive in your marital relationship. Paul writes in Philippians 4:8, "Whatever is true, whatever is honorable, whatever is just, whatever is pure, whatever is pleasing, whatever is commendable, if there is any excellence and if there is anything worthy of praise, think about these things." When this is the attitude of a husband and wife, there is continual encouragement for each to be their very best. Problems and difficulties can better be confronted and more readily resolved with positive attitudes. The way something is said with a loving attitude becomes as important as what is said. For example, rather than saying, "That is the dumbest idea I have ever heard;" it is better to say, "I know you have given good thought to this. Help me understand your reasoning that led you to this position."

This principle also helps a couple anticipate the good instead of assuming the negative. Instead of asking, "How was your day?", which is usually answered with one word like frustrating, horrible, crazy, or fine. A better response will be given to a question like, "Tell me what was the most interesting thing that happened in your day?" Or "What did you learn today that was helpful to you?" or "What did you do for someone today?" Questions like these usually lead to meaningful conversations because there is a genuine interest expressed in your mate's activities during the day. Thoughtful words and the way we use them make a world of difference in marriage talk. Leave behind the childish claim that, "Sticks and stones may break my bones, but words can never hurt me." Be assured that words can be a blessing, or weapons of pain. Always try to choose words that make your daily TALK affirming, positive, loving, and interesting for your mate.

THE FOURTH "T" IS TOUCH

Love in marriage needs touch just as a healthy body needs sleep. Non-sexual touching and kissing are ways to put love into action. Touching your mate with kindness and affection strengthens the bond of marriage. It affirms each other as the one you love and enjoy. Through personal touch we experience comfort, pleasure, and encouragement. It is not surprising that often we read in the New Testament Gospels about men, women, and children who reached out to touch Jesus our Lord with the hope He would touch them. The touch of love is a great gift.

It didn't take long for Sandra and me to learn the joy of touch. On our second date we discovered that our lips were a perfect match. I clearly remember we were taking a stroll on the beach at St. Simons Island in Georgia. The moon was full and shinning a yellow path from the ocean's horizon to the edge of the water where we were walking. We couldn't resist our first kiss. Ever since that romantic evening Sandra and I enjoy sharing kisses to indicate how important we are to each other. It is our nature to kiss each other often, especially when we leave the house, when we return, and when we are about to go to sleep. Our kisses are acts of thoughtfulness and expressions of our love. They are fun and we like the little tingle we often feel when we kiss.

Greeting each other with a kiss is a great feeling when you return home from work, or from a trip. It is one of the ways we practice our wedding day promise, "To love, honor, and cherish each other for as long as we both shall live." We show we cherish each other by enjoying a hug and a kiss. I remember hearing a husband during a marriage seminar say, "The time I feel most loved is when I come home to my wife. She seems so excited to see me. She hurries to the door with a big smile and gives me a kiss. It makes me look forward to coming home every day."

Touch is also a way to be playful with each other. Giving the "high five" is a way of agreeing or celebrating a happy moment. Bumping each other as you pass by, or touching your mate's back as you walk through a room when others are present are nonverbal ways of saying, "I like you." Playing footsie under the table at a restaurant with a smile on your face lets your mate know you are aware of this special time of being together. In more private places tickling each other, without over doing it, is a fun way to touch. It produces laughter and helps release stress and frustration. It can also be a test of trust. Ask your mate to close his or her eyes, lift their arms, and try not to laugh. Just wait and see what happens!

One of the most loving gifts you can give your husband or wife is a back rub, a foot massage, or running your fingers through their hair providing you have permission. These acts of touching can be more effective than words or gifts in communicating love. Studies of happy marriages always list frequent touching as one of the primary reasons. This includes holding hands in public, sitting close where arms and legs touch, adjusting each other's clothes when something is out of place like a shirt tag, and giving each other a hand to avoid a fall.

The familiar saying, "Reach out and touch someone today" is profoundly true for a husband and wife to include in their daily activity. The following poem about hugs by Jill Wolf reminds us of the value of human touch.

"There's something in a simple hug that always warms the heart;
It welcomes us back home and makes it easier to part.
A hug's a way to share the joy and sad times we go through,
Or just a way for friends to say they like you cause you're you.
A hug is an amazing thing – It's just the perfect way
To show the love we're feeling, but can't find the words to say.
It's funny how a little hug makes everyone feel good;
In every place and language it's always understood.
And hugs don't need equipment, special batteries or parts –
Just open up your arms and open up your heart."

THE FIFTH "T" IS THANKS

When someone gives "thanks" for you, it is a powerful boost to your sense of self-worth. Mary Martin demonstrated this during her first performance in "South Pacific" on a New York Broadway stage. Just before the show began, she received a note from the famous operatic manager Oscar Hammerstein, who at the time was on his deathbed. He wanted her to know how <u>thankful</u> he was for her musical talents and for their friendship. The short note simply said, "Dear Mary! A bell's not a bell till you ring it. A song's not a song till you sing it. Love in your heart is not put there to stay. Love isn't love till you give it away."

After the play that evening, many people rushed backstage to praise Mary for her singing and acting. They asked her, "What happened to you while you were on stage tonight? We've never seen such an outstanding performance." Blinking back the tears of joy, Mary read them the note from Hammerstein. Then she said, "Tonight, I gave my love away!"

Just like Mary Martin's experience after receiving the note of "Thanks" and encouragement from her friend that night, the self-esteem of a husband and wife is greatly enhanced when genuine "thanks" is expressed for each other. Since it is so valuable for each other's well-being, a husband and wife should give this "T" to each other every day. My spirit is always lifted when my wife, Sandra, signs a note or card to me with the words, "I am so thankful for you." When we are praying together and she expresses thanks to God for me, my heart is warmed. When I hear her complimenting my ministry in front of other people, my motivation to do my best is increased even more.

In similar ways, I have regularly expressed appreciation for Sandra to God and others. I do not take for granted her many talents, thoughtful ways, and most importantly her authenticity. I openly recognize them with praise. I can truthfully say with Solomon who wrote Proverbs 31, "A capable wife...is far more precious than jewels. She does him good and not harm all the days of her life. Strength and dignity are her clothing, and the teaching of kindness is on her tongue. She looks well to the ways of her household. Her children rise up and call her blessed; her husband too, and he praises her. Charm is deceitful, and beauty is vain, but a woman who honors the Lord is to be praised."

Even though every husband and wife admit shortcomings and mistakes, an abiding awareness of each being God's gift should bring forth thanksgiving every day of marriage. When this kind of thanks for each other is expressed in meaningful ways, true love continues to grow stronger in their relationship. Appreciation is a gift for the heart that exceeds the value of other tangible treasures.

These "Five T's of Marriage", therefore, are daily requirements for a happy and healthy marriage. Just as doctors recommend daily vitamins to keep the body strong, the "Five T's" give marriage the energy and power to complete the journey with abundant satisfaction. Do your best to activate TRUST, TIME, TALK, TOUCH, and THANKS every day of your marriage.

CHAPTER FOURTEEN

A CONTRACT FOR FIGHTING FAIR

Ephesians 4: 26 & 29, *"Be angry but do not sin; do not let the sun go down on your anger. Let no evil talk come out of your mouths, but only what is useful for building up, as there is need, so that your words may give grace to those who hear."*

During a weekend road trip, a married couple stopped at a restaurant for lunch. After enjoying a good meal and visiting the restrooms, they resumed their drive toward the mountain cottage where they planned to spend a few days. After about thirty minutes from the restaurant, the wife cried out, "O my God! I left my glasses in the restroom." This did not make her husband a happy camper. He began chastising her for being so careless. Allowing his angry mood to escalate, he accused her of "always forgetting something." He found a place where he could turn the car around, and they unhappily began driving back to retrieve the glasses.

All the way back to the restaurant, the husband fussed about losing time because of her carelessness. The more he complained, the angrier she became. The more she defended herself, the more he blamed her for ruining their weekend that was supposed to be a fun get-a-way. Just before she got out of the car to get her glasses, he said, "While you are in there, you might as well get my hat I left in the chair, and my credit card that is by the register."

This couple obviously had a fight in the car, but he didn't fight fair. He was unkind to his wife because <u>she</u> made a mistake. He blamed her for ruining the weekend when <u>his</u> bad attitude was the real problem. He wasn't honest during his complaining because he didn't admit he also had left two things in the restaurant. He exaggerated and overstated the mistake by saying, "you always forget something." Finally, and more unacceptable was his failure to treat her the way he would want to be treated. All of this unpleasantness could have been avoided if they had previously written "A Contract For Fighting Fair," and then activated their agreements to resolve their conflict.

Conflicts are inevitable. Every married couple has disagreements. The important issue is not to become "disagreeable." The goal of a husband and wife during these times should be to listen to each other with respect and understanding, and to seek a solution, or at least a satisfactory compromise. Arguments should be off limits because they always produce a "winner" and a "loser". Every married couple knows it is no fun to live with either. Arguments are a contest in which both parties present carefully worded statements intended to appeal to the good sense of reason and logic. The implication is obvious: anyone who does not agree with my argument is an unreasonable person. When this path is taken during a conflict, damage is done to the marital relationship.

The better path to take in order to resolve disagreements is to follow a carefully prepared contract for fighting fair. This is one of the assignments I have given to several thousand couples during their premarital counseling sessions. I provide them with a work sheet listing some of my suggestions. Then after they carefully discuss and write out their <u>agreements</u> for seeking solutions to their future misunderstandings and times of anger, I ask them to sign and date their contract. I sign it with them as a Pastor and friend to validate their pledge to follow the rules they have set for themselves. I remind them that their contract is a living document. They can change it, add to it, amend it, and delete certain rules as their marriage develops. But they are to follow the agreements as long as it is current. They are to hold each other accountable to practice and live up to their "Contract For Fighting Fair." Jokingly I tell them they can call upon me (except during the middle of the night) to be a witness of their signatures. I will verify that indeed they **agreed to resolve** differing opinions in responsible ways instead of arguing like quarreling children.

This contract should include agreements they will follow when they experience anger, disagreements, and hurt feelings. It also should list things they will not do or say during these times. The scripture beginning this chapter from Ephesians 4:29 gives Godly counsel by saying, "Let no evil talk come out of your mouths, but only what is useful for building up, as there is need, so that your words may give grace to those who hear."

The following are some suggestions and specific points of agreement husbands and wives should follow in resolving their problems.

A CONTRACT FOR FIGHTING FAIR

1. We will obey God's Word in Ephesians 5:26, "Be angry, but do not sin; do not let the sun go down on your anger." We, therefore, will not go to bed at night angry.
2. We will discuss our difference without arguing by selecting a private place to talk:
   A. We will not talk at the same time, raise our voices, or interrupt each other.
   B. The first to speak will state the issue and talk calmly, honestly, and considerately.
   C. The listener will hear with good body language, understand, and repeat what was heard.
   D. Then the roles are reversed following the rules in B & C.
   E. A time out will be honored if either needs to take a break to avoid arguing.
   F. Compromises, accommodations, and apologies will conclude the discussion in love.
3. Even when angry, we will remember and keep our marriage promises to love, honor, and cherish each other. We will, therefore, work toward a win-win solution when there is a problem. In our marriage we don't want to have a winner and a loser. We will fight fair over <u>what</u> is right and wrong and not <u>who</u> is right or wrong. We will avoid getting personal and accusing each other. We will stay focused on the issue or problem being discussed and seek a solution.
4. Every day we will live by Jesus' Golden Rule in The Gospel of Matthew 7:12, which is: "Do unto others as you would have them do unto you." We will do for and talk to each other in the ways we would want for ourselves.
5. We will memorize Philippians 4: 4-7, and often say it privately and as a couple. These superlative words will give us the seven gifts of the Holy Spirit which are: REJOICING instead of despairing, GENTLENESS instead of anger, OUR LORD'S PRESENCE instead of loneliness, CONFIDENCE instead of anxiety, PRAYER instead of doubt, THANKSGIVING instead of complaining, and PEACE instead of confusion.

6. We will be realistic and accept the fact that life is hard. We will not expect everything in our relationship and in our home to be always free of problems and frustrations. We will look for lessons we can learn and ways in which we can mature from painful and unjust experiences.

7. We can share our anger and frustration according to the guidelines above, but we will never hit each other, throw things, or break anything in our home when upset.

8. We will identify offensive words and agree never to speak them in our home even when angry.

9. When confronted with a problem, we will avoid rushing to assumptions that may not be correct. We, therefore, will ask questions to clarify disagreements and listen empathetically for better understanding. We then can respond more wisely instead of with a quick emotional reaction.

10. We will not bring up the past. After we have dealt with a problem and forgiven each other, we will not bring it up during a future disagreement to discredit each other. God's love enables us to remember what is positive and good in order to avoid being negative about past mistakes.

11. We will not use the "silent treatment" on each other, or pout when we have a disagreement.

12. We will use "I" messages, instead of "you" messages. This means we will take responsibility for our feelings, what we like and don't like, and discuss issues with the first person pronoun. We will not use the second person pronoun to blame the other. We will say, "I don't like..." instead of "You are so inconsiderate..."

13. We will take each other's views seriously, even when we disagree without being sarcastic or condescending. We will never demean or verbally harm one another with our anger.

14. We will state our views and disagreements as honestly as possible without exaggerating. We will avoid saying "always" and "never." These words usually overstate the problem.

15. We will not criticize each other in front of others, but only behind closed doors.

16. When we make a mistake and disappoint each other, we will quickly apologize and ask for forgiveness with the promise to not let it happen again. We promise to always forgive by God's Grace when an apology is given. We then will let it go, put it behind us, and get happy again.

17. We will seek God's Will when we are faced with important matters that we can't readily resolve. We will do this by praying, searching the scriptures, and seeking righteous counsel from others.

18. We will never threaten each other with leaving or divorcing. We will live in hope even during the worst of times and wait upon God to guide us through days of conflict.

19. We will maintain confidentiality about our personal differences. We will not discuss them with family members, friends, or colleagues at work unless we give each other permission to do so.

20. We will review this contract at least once a quarter and evaluate "THE STATE OF OUR UNION." We will try to remember the number for each item in our contract so when either of us fails to live up to an agreement, we can remind each other by number in a fun and playful way.

21. If we reach an impasse with a problem, or experience what seems to be an irreconcilable difference, we will seek "righteous counsel" as the Bible directs us to do. We will not prolong the problem by ignoring it. We will promptly go "together" and allow a Christian Counselor or Pastor to guide us toward new insights and better communication in resolving our differences.

_____   _____
Husband's Signature   Wife's Signature

_____
Pastor's Signature as the Witness

_____
Date

    This contract can set positive boundaries for couples to confront problems in honest and loving ways. It can help them avoid doing and saying harmful things that otherwise will create bitterness and resentment. Fights are going to happen in marriages; there is no way two unique and different people can get around them. Therefore, choose to "Fight Fair" and solve the disagreements that evolve in marriage. Seek to build up your marriage by doing the right thing instead of letting selfishness, stubbornness, and anger tear it down.

One of the best ways to equip your marriage for difficult times is with the words of God from the Holy Bible. Some of these passages that give Divine Counsel for marriage are:

1. "Trust in the Lord with all your heart, and do not rely on your own insight. In all your ways acknowledge Him, and He will make straight your paths" Proverbs 3: 5-6.
2. "You must understand this, my beloved: let everyone be quick to listen, slow to speak, slow to anger; for your anger does not produce God's righteousness" James 1: 19-20.
3. "An anxious heart weighs a person down, but a kind word cheers him up" Proverbs 12: 25.
4. "The heart of the righteous ponders how to answer, but the mouth of the wicked pours out harmful things." Proverbs 15: 28.
5. "A wise person's heart guides his mouth, and his lips promote persuasiveness. Pleasant words are a honeycomb, sweet to the soul and healing to the bones." Proverbs 16: 23–24.
6. "A person finds joy in a fitting answer, and how delightful is a timely word." Proverbs 15: 23.
7. "If I understand all mysteries and have all knowledge, but do not have love, I am nothing...Love is patient and kind; love does not insist on its own way; love is not irritable or resentful; it does not rejoice in the wrong, but rejoices in what is right and true. Love bears all things, believes all things, hopes all things, and endures all things... Love never ends. Faith, hope, and love abide, but the greatest of these is love" I Corinthians 13.

Always remember that marriage is given by God for a man and woman who become one flesh even though they are two very different people. It is both a mystery and a divine relationship. God who instituted marriage from the beginning of creation knows exactly what it takes for this union to bring happiness and fulfillment. God reveals this knowledge through His Eternal Word. Therefore, when conflict comes in marriage, hear and do God's Word from Ephesians 4:26 & 29: "Be angry but do not sin; do not let the sun go down on your anger. Let no evil talk come out of your mouths, but only what is useful for building up, as there is need, so that your words may give grace to those who hear."

CHAPTER FIFTEEN

BY GOD'S GRACE

John 1: 14, 16, *"The Word became flesh and lived among us, and we have seen His Glory, the Glory as of a father's only son, full of Grace and Truth... From His fullness we have all received, Grace upon Grace."*

Grace is receiving what we do not deserve.
Justice is receiving what we do deserve.
Mercy is not receiving what we do deserve.

Grace is God's unmerited, unearned blessings and kindness. It is because God is by nature the eternal essence of pure love that we receive His favor through faith in Jesus Christ. "From His fullness we have all received, Grace upon Grace" (John 1: 16). The reason we can be gracious to others, especially in marriage, is because we each have received a bountiful supply of God's Grace.

This Grace enables imperfect husbands and wives who are united in the covenant of Christian marriage to fulfill their promises of faithfulness even when things go wrong. By God's grace, they can successfully share life as best friends and partners <u>regardless of the circumstances</u> that come and go. Someone has rightly said that grace is the oil which lessens the friction of marriage. It smoothes out the rough places and keeps the many responsibilities of home life functioning in harmony like a well lubricated clock.

Sandra and I learned our first lesson about this marital grace on our honeymoon. Our wedding was in her home town of Hinesville, Georgia, September 23, 1967. The ceremony at the Hinesville First Methodist

Church was beautiful and inspiring. The reception featured about 400 happy people, delicious food, flowers, and dynamic music. The fun, excitement, and best wishes from our family and friends sent us off with a wonderful start to become husband and wife. Early that evening, we left the Church ecstatic with joy and began driving in my 1965 two tone Impala hardtop to Ashville, North Carolina. We had bought an all-inclusive honeymoon package at the historic Grove Park Inn. The next morning as the light began to shine through our bedroom windows, I turned toward Sandra for a good morning kiss. She looked at me with a startled expression, giggled, put her hand over her mouth, and asked, "Do you look this way every morning?" Admittedly my hair was all messed up, my face was unshaven, and my breath was less than desirable. In order to ease her disappointment, I said, "Sandra, sit up. We need to discuss the meaning of grace." I knew it would take a lot of grace for her to live with me every day.

We then went downstairs to eat breakfast. It was an elegant dining room. From the door, you could see dishes and silverware properly placed on designer tablecloths with cloth napkins at each place setting. The *maitre d'* standing tall in his black tuxedo greeted us at the door with a formal welcome to the Grove Park Inn. He then sternly informed me that I could not be served without a tie. I was shocked. I responded with a strong explanation that this was the first day of our honeymoon. I explained we had already paid for our meals and lodging. I then with some passion said, "It is eight o'clock in the morning. No one in their right mind while on their honeymoon wears a tie to breakfast!" Without flinching, he made zero effort to accommodate my tieless attire.

Sandra interceded at that point and took me by the hand. We stepped out into the hallway. She then said, "Jim, we need to discuss the meaning of grace." I then took a deep breath, smiled, and apologized. I hurried upstairs to get my tie. When I returned, I had a grin on my face and a bright tie around the neck of my sport shirt. The Maitre d' smiled and welcomed us again to the Grove Park dining room. I extended my right arm to Sandra and we made our grand entrance into the dining hall on what seemed to be a silk carpet of grace.

We didn't get through the first day of marriage without learning that grace is needed to get past the annoying and negative incidents of life. Acts of grace extend undeserved favor and kindness! It has a wonderful way of making things better and getting things moving again in the right direction. Together we have been learning how to give and receive grace for more than forty three years. Every day, it proves to be the one essential gift of God that keeps harmony in our marriage. We are continuing to learn that grace enables us to grow in three major areas of our marriage while overcoming pride, stubbornness, and selfishness.

FIRST, GRACE GIVES US THE MOTIVATION TO DELIGHT IN EACH OTHER

Every person has the secret desire to be known as they really are without any pretense and to be loved for just being their self. Grace is the means for this to happen. A husband and wife know each other better than any other person in their lives. They know each other first-hand: the beautiful and the ugly, the good and the bad, and the positive and the negative. Grace makes possible their delighting in each other while making <u>allowances</u> for differences and imperfections. This is what is so amazing about Grace. Just as we are received by God through His Grace and loved as His sons and daughters because of our faith in Jesus Christ, we too are able to love each other with patience. It is not that we condone wrong behavior and attitude, but that in spite of each other's mistakes and weaknesses, we continue in our relationship of marriage patiently seeking to make things right by God's Grace. More than just tolerating each other, this Grace allows us to enjoy one another and to delight in each other's presence.

This is true because Christian marriages bring to men and women more fulfillment and happiness than any other relationship, position, or possession. They promote better health and longer lives, the result for couples who allow Grace to keep their love alive. Surveys continue to confirm that the estimated contributions for marriage meet the needs of men and women more than all other kinds of satisfaction.

Many books have been written about the basic needs of women and men. In general, women seek acceptance, caring, understanding, reassurance, thoughtfulness, loyalty, and security. Some of the basic needs of men are sexual satisfaction, respect, appreciation, patience, admiration, trust, and encouragement. Knowing these basic needs enable a husband and wife to make extra efforts in fulfilling them. Even when you don't feel like it or are too occupied with your own interests, Grace reminds you to do your best to be sensitive to your mate's needs and seek to provide satisfaction as you would want to be pleased.

Grace helps men delight in their wives by giving them frequent hugs. Someone has calculated that most women want at least four hugs a day. Other acts of Grace include warming her car on a cold day, opening a door for her, leaving a "Have a Happy Day Note" where she will see it the first thing in the morning, completing a chore she normally does, arranging a surprise night out, and giving her a full body massage without charge.

Grace also motivates women to compliment their husbands unexpectedly. These are emotional hugs that men appreciate. Both husbands and wives discover the power of Grace to discipline the tongue, to avoid criticisms, and to curb unnecessary sarcasm. It promotes positive attitudes, seeks solutions, and enables cooperation. It increases affection for each other through touching, holding hands, kissing, and being playful with each other even in public.

SECOND, GRACE ENABLES US TO SUPPORT EACH OTHER

God's Grace is freely given to husbands and wives who will receive it and share it with each other. It is the means of giving each other support in good and bad times. It avoids making the small and insignificant issues of daily living major problems. Even if you would have said or done something differently than your mate, it is more loving to take your mate's side on most matters. Instead of pronouncing judgment that is void of support, asking an appropriate question for "clarification" (try this) is a better way of responding. Grace is the guidance that provides a steady stream of small acts of kindness.

For example, if a wife has experienced a disagreement with a friend in which she defended her actions by charging her with the same behavior, the husband should not scold her by saying, "You shouldn't have done that." Instead, his support should express understanding of her frustration and anger. Then he could say, "Your friendship with her means a lot to you. What can you do to let her know your intentions were not to upset her?" In a response like this, Grace seeks the positive side of daily situations. It isn't the easiest way to live. It is just the best way to maintain peace and unity in marriage.

One of the best lessons of Grace I ever learned was from Bernie and Freida. I became their pastor in 1970. After Sandra and I became good friends with them, they told us the story of a failed plumbing business that led them into bankruptcy. After 25 years of marriage and without children, Bernie decided to try his entrepreneurial skills. Frieda was not as enthusiastic about this new venture as Bernie. However, when it proved to be highly successful, Frieda encouraged him to expand for greater profits. Their business prospered until a housing slump brought their plumbing company to a standstill. Realizing they had overextended themselves financially, they had no choice but to declare bankruptcy.

It was a most difficult time for them and their marriage. Frieda was inclined to blame Bernie for risking everything they had to start the company. Bernie claimed they could have avoided failure if Frieda hadn't insisted on expanding the business after it became so successful. When they were at their lowest point and realizing the negative impact this problem was having on their marriage, they called upon the Lord to give them hope. Somehow the Grace of God awakened them to the fact that their relationship as husband and wife was far more important than making money. By God's grace, Bernie decided he and Frieda needed to go on a vacation to renew their love, to get some needed rest, and to give God the opportunity to direct their future. They remembered God's promise in Proverbs 3: 5-6, "Trust in the Lord with all your heart, and do not rely on your own insight. In all your ways, acknowledge Him, and He will make straight your paths." Bernie had a great sense of humor and he told me, "We got off the straight path — greed led us down a rocky and crooked path to nowhere. We humbled ourselves before God, and asked Him to show us the way He wanted us to go."

Do you want to know what Bernie did next? He went to the local bank and asked for a $500 loan. He knew the president of the bank personally. He was astonished that Bernie had the audacity to ask for a loan in the midst of bankruptcy. Bernie explained with his usual grin, "Hey, if Frieda and I are going to get back on our feet and pay our creditors what we owe, we need to have some fun. We need the loan to take a vacation on the beach in Florida." The president provided him the money and was amazed that it was returned in full with interest after six months. After their vacation (which they claimed was the best one they ever had), they were able to take over a women's apparel store on Main Street that was failing. Frieda, who was very stylish and Bernie, who was an excellent businessman, made a great team. Together by the Grace of God they overcame the "blame game" after failing in the plumbing business. They renewed their marriage with loving support for each other. After a few years of success, they were able to pay all the money they owed to previous creditors and began realizing significant profits for themselves.

Who would have ever thought that a vacation was the answer to their despair? Many would say "They had failed in business, and didn't deserve a trip to Florida." Yet they understood that God's Grace doesn't give us what we deserve. Grace provides <u>what will bless us,</u> and give us a new beginning. By faith in Jesus Christ, Bernie and Frieda experienced what the Gospel of John reports in Chapter One, "In Him was life, and the life was the light of all people. The light shines in the darkness, and the darkness did not overcome it...From His fullness we have received *grace upon grace."*

THIRD, GRACE MAKES POSSIBLE OUR FORGIVING EACH OTHER

We live in an imperfect world. Sin and selfishness corrupted God's creation which He had pronounced "Good." God's Divine Ideal for marriage was for there to be harmony and perfect love in the union of a husband and wife. Sin and selfishness made it otherwise. Grace has been given, therefore, to remedy the marital dilemma of mistakes and disharmony. Grace enables a husband and wife to forgive each other and restore their relationship when it is damaged by wrong. Marriage cannot live without forgiveness. Our promises when we marry are not prior accomplishments. We only pledge our intentions to be faithful in sickness and in health, in joy and in sorrow, and in plenty and in want. We can only seek to do our best as we mature in our marital love. We know there will be times of disappointment, failure, hurt, and mistakes. Our vows, therefore, are contingent upon the Grace of God making our forgiveness of each other possible when we have no other course to take. The great English statesman, Sir Winston Churchill, knew this was true about marriage when he said, "Wars are not won by evacuation. Neither are marriages saved by bailing out."

Forgiveness is the answer, and grace is the gift that pardons wrongdoing. Christians are daily conscious that "It is by Grace we each have been saved" (Ephesians 2:8). The words of Jesus in Matthew Chapter 6 are clear: "Forgive us our trespasses as we forgive those who have trespassed against us...For if you forgive others their trespasses, your heavenly Father will also forgive you, but if you do not forgive others, neither will your Father forgive your trespasses." Jesus' disciple, Peter, asked Him one day, "Lord, if a brother sins against me, how often should I forgive? As many as seven times?" Jesus said to him, "Not seven times, but, I tell you, seventy-seven times" (Matthew 18:21 – 22). The Apostle Paul emphasized Jesus' teaching about forgiveness in the very heart of his letters to the Churches of the first century as in Ephesians 4: 32 – 5: 2, "Be kind to one another, tenderhearted, forgiving one another, as God in Christ has forgiven you. Therefore be imitators of God, as beloved children, and live in love, as Christ loved us and gave Himself up for us."

Christian marriage is, therefore, to be a unique display of God's Covenant Grace extended to the entire world. It is a showcase of love, grace, forgiveness, mercy, and reconciliation. People who do not know the Love of God and the Grace of Jesus Christ can learn from a Christian marriage the nature of God's Kingdom on earth as it is in heaven. There it is evident that Grace gives peace and unity when human flaws, imperfections, and mistakes would otherwise bring discord. Perhaps the most frequent words heard in Christian marriages are, "I love you, I am sorry, please forgive me, I forgive you, and let's try again."

The backside of Grace is humor. Grace makes it possible for us not to take ourselves and each other too seriously. The ability to laugh at ourselves even in frustrating situations enables us to keep things in balance with a positive perspective on life. It also helps us lower our expectations of each other in marriage. Only God can ultimately meet our deepest needs of love, joy, hope, and peace. When we understand that Grace can enable us to make allowances for each other, we then can forgive in times of disappointment. For example, a husband asked his wife, "Why can't you cook biscuits like my mother used to?" Knowing she was not his mother and refusing to take his comment personally, she responded with a logical reason. She said, "I don't cook biscuits like your mother because you don't bring home the dough like your daddy did!" When they realized how ridiculous their comments to each other were, they were able to laugh.

Even though humor is helpful at times to prevent a grievance from becoming a major problem, forgiveness is not easy. It first of all takes grace to realize our mistakes and shortcomings so we can offer reconciliation to others. Then it takes patience, time, and a lot of effort. Forgiveness is not the same as forgetting. It doesn't mean a "change of memory": it means a change of <u>heart</u>. It does not overlook or condone wrong, but it recognizes that people we love are more important than their faults and mistakes. Forgiveness allows the offender to have another chance, even many chances as Jesus instructed us to provide. And for the forgiver, grace frees us from harboring bitterness and seeking revenge.

The divine effects of God's Grace are realized in the story of a wife who couldn't take the neglect of her husband anymore. She finally informed her counselor that she was filing for a divorce. She said, "Life is all about him and his career. I feel useless and unwanted. I am deeply hurt, and I want to see the hurt in his face when I present him with divorce papers." The counselor was sad to hear her decision. She then presented a proposal that she had used successfully with other failed marriages.

She said, "If you divorce him now, it won't hurt him very much because he is already oblivious to you. I would like to suggest that for the next six months you refuse to be a victim and become an alluring woman of many gifts. Pamper him with thoughtful acts. Seek to meet his every need. Give of yourself in generous ways that cause him to think you adore him day and night. Then after six months of showering him with loving attention, present him with the divorce papers. That will surprise him and hurt him as nothing else could. It will be like pulling the rug out from under him as you watch him fall."

The unfulfilled wife liked this plan. She immediately set out to accomplish her objective by proving to her husband how wonderful she could be! Over the next six months, he was enamored with her loving and thoughtful care. The strategy was far more successful than she dreamed it could be. His desire to be with her increased dramatically. She began to discover again what a wonderful man he was, and how important she felt with his generous attention for her wellbeing.

Instead of keeping the appointment that she made with the counselor six months ago, she called to report that the divorce was off. The counselor was intrigued with this news and asked for the details that cancelled the divorce. After the woman joyfully described the changes that she and her husband experienced, the counselor said, "This is what I was hoping for. The plan to act with undeserved love has worked again. Isn't it amazing what 'Amazing Grace' can do?"

CHAPTER SIXTEEN

HOW DO YOU LISTEN?

Mark 4: 2-9, *"Jesus began to teach them many things in parables, and in His teaching He said to them: 'Listen! A sower went out to sow. And as he sowed, some seed fell on the path, and the birds came and ate it up. Other seed fell on rocky ground, where it did not have much soil, and it sprang up quickly, since it had no depth of soil. And when the sun rose, it was scorched; and since it had no root, it withered away. Other seed fell among thorns, and the thorns grew up and choked it, and it yielded no grain. Other seed fell into good soil and brought forth grain, growing up and increasing and yielding thirty and sixty and a hundredfold.' And He said, 'Let anyone with ears to hear listen!'"*

This scripture from the Gospel of Mark records an historic moment in the ministry of Jesus Christ. It is the beginning of His teaching with parables. He chose the shore by The Sea of Galilee. I have been there eight times, and it is my favorite place of natural beauty to visit in all of Israel. Parables became Jesus' unique way of communicating the heavenly truths of God in visual stories people could easily understand and remember.

The first parable He told is printed above. It is called "The Parable of The Sower." Its subject is listening. He could have selected many topics of eternal importance to begin His teaching with parables. However, the one He considered most important emphasized the responsibility of people hearing the Truth and allowing it to be productive in their lives. Just as hearing the Gospel produces faith that leads to salvation, so listening in marriage is essential for love to grow and be shared in a marriage.

Unfortunately, a husband or wife hears what is being said, but often fails to listen to the message of the heart. An example of this is when a wife one morning told her husband of a strange dream she had during the night. She said, "Honey, I had the most wonderful dream about you placing a beautiful gold necklace around my neck on Valentine's Day. What do you think a dream like that means?"

He answered with some confusion, "I honestly don't know. Dreams can really be mysterious."

After a few more mornings, she told him it happened again. She said, "I had another dream that was so clear and delightful. I saw the same necklace up closer. It had a special heart charm that was 14 carat gold. What do you think it could possibly mean?"

He said, "That is really interesting. I have no idea what your dream means."

Two days before Valentines' Day, she was so excited about having another dream. She told her husband that during the night she saw the gold chain necklace with the gold heart. She said, "This time it had a diamond in the center. It was absolutely beautiful. Sweetheart, what do you think this third dream could mean?"

He replied, "Well, Valentines' Day will soon be here. Maybe we can find an answer to your dreams then." He realized he had better get to the store and do something about her night visions.

On Valentines' Evening, she prepared a romantic dinner for them to enjoy. Soft music was playing and the dining room was lit with candles. She gave him a wrapped gift that contained a new shirt he could wear golfing. He then presented her with a beautifully wrapped present. She eagerly opened it with childlike anticipation. The last thing she expected was a book! The title was "The Meaning of Dreams."

He may have heard what she was saying, but he wasn't listening to her heart's desire. He could have benefited from Jesus' parable about the importance of true listening. The parable opens with the call to listen. The last word of the parable is also "listen." It is not enough to just hear the words being said. Jesus says we have an essential responsibility to listen to the message of what is being said with interest and understanding. Jesus, therefore, would be the first to say that if we want a dynamic and strong marriage that will endure the long journey of life, listening is the key.

Jesus masterfully teaches this in "The Parable of The Sower." Although the main purpose of this teaching concerns hearing the Truth of God's Word and then acting upon it with fruitful living, it is most relevant to the health of marriage. Jesus knew that there are four ways of hearing, but only one of them makes productive listening possible. He compares these four kinds of hearing with the four kinds of soil found on the land in Israel. In His parable, the sower is the one who is presenting the message to be heard. The seed is the message of truth seeking to be heard and acted upon. In regard to marriage, the message is often about personal feelings and concerns, desires and dreams, joys and sorrows, needs and requests, and hurts and hopes of a husband and wife.

THE FIRST KIND OF HEARING: LISTENING WITH A CLOSED HEART

Jesus compared this way of hearing with a path hardened by the many people and animals that daily walked upon it. When the seed fell on this ground it did not enter the soil. It remained on the surface where birds gladly fed upon the available food. This analogy is like words falling on deaf ears. It means there is no personal engagement with the message, no meaningful response, and certainly no productive action. The sower or the one who is speaking is essentially ignored. The words are wasted. There is no real communication.

This was the case after a year of marriage when a young wife surprised her husband with a new hairdo. It was to be a special evening celebrating their first wedding anniversary. Reservations had been made at one of their favorite restaurants. Leading up to that day, she spent hours looking at different hair styles in magazines and catalogues. Then it took over an hour for the beautician to cut and style her hair according to the design she chose. She was very pleased with the results, and could hardly wait for her husband to see her new look. When he came in from work, she rushed to him and asked, "What do you think?" He took a casual glance, and said, "You look fine. Let's go eat now. I'm starved." It was not a good evening for them. His hard and uncaring heart broke hers because he did not listen to the verbal and nonverbal words she was saying. He simply did not get the message.

THE SECOND KIND OF HEARING: LISTENING WITH A ME-ISM HEART

Jesus said this kind of hearing is like rocky ground that didn't have any depth to the soil. The seed sown in such soil spring up quickly, but soon die when the sun withers them. The soil is fertile, but there is a layer of rock just beneath the surface of this kind of ground. The soil is so shallow the roots of the young plants cannot go deep enough to reach moisture.

This illustrates hearing that is not receptive to the opinions of others or to learning new things. It is selfish hearing that is fixated on a me-ism heart. The bottom line of this kind of hearing reveals there isn't enough room in this soil for anyone else but me. Superficial interest is shown occasionally, like the seed that grows quickly. But a marriage relationship does not grow into meaningful communication if this is the only level of hearing.

This was the case with Bill and Betty. Bill accepted the responsibility of managing the family budget and paying all the bills. After months of frustration, seeing credit card charges exceed income, he asked Betty to discuss this matter with him. She satisfied him with quick promises to do better, but the bills for the next three months indicated she had not taken the matter seriously. Her response had been shallow, and her intentions to discipline her excessive buying were canceled by her selfish interests. Betty's unwillingness to hear Bill's plea for restrained spending caused dissatisfaction in other areas of their marriage. It was not just a disagreement about managing money. The issue was realizing how troubling this was to Bill and seeing the trust level decrease in their partnership. It was only after the problem got worse, and Bill and Betty received marital counseling that Betty admitted her selfish life style. She at first told the counselor, "I didn't think it was a big deal." Later she confessed ignoring Bill's request for help and cooperation and her denial of reality regarding their credit standing with the bank. Her me-ism hearing was replaced with new listening skills with the perspective that their marriage was about "us" and not just about "me and my personal wants."

THE THIRD KIND OF HEARING: LISTENING WITH AN OCCUPIED HEART

Jesus description of this third level of hearing is very familiar to most of us, especially to men. It is called selective hearing. It is like good soil that allows most anything to grow. Even when productive seed is sown into it, little effort is made to keep out the weeds and thorny bushes. As a result, so many maverick plants begin to grow that the good seed does not have enough room to survive. In these conditions they are crowded out, and prevented from developing the harvest they are capable of producing.

This hearing is only partial listening. Someone is talking and wanting the attention of the listener but little eye contact is given. The body language indicates other distractions and activities are compromising the full meaning of what is being said. The speaker, therefore, begins to shutdown because there is a growing awareness the listener's attention is being divided by other matters.

Throughout our marriage, Sandra has often confronted me with having this kind of listening. As she is talking to me, my mind seems to her to be wandering, and not paying attention. She observes me doing other things as she talks, and not giving her my undivided attention. I have tried to convince her that men by nature are "multi-tasked persons." Men can listen carefully, and hear every word that is being said while opening the mail, changing channels on the TV, talking on the cell phone, and enjoying a refreshing drink. However, she isn't buying my explanation. She is not impressed with multi-tasked people. When she is talking, she believes I should be looking at her with certain expressions of interest. She wants me to stop doing the many things that to her seem distracting. She wants me to respond with more than a grunt to what she is saying. In other words, my wife wants me to clear out all the weeds and thorny bushes in my mind when she is talking. She believes effective and loving listening means taking her seriously, discontinuing secondary activities, and giving her first place in my interests. She occasionally reminds me that I did promise on our wedding day to love, honor, and cherish her by forsaking all others (which includes competing distractions) so she will know she is number one in my heart. As difficult as it is for me, I am learning to accept the fact that she doesn't appreciate my great ability to multi-task while she is speaking. The selective hearing with an occupied heart just doesn't cut it with her. She even believes I should practice the kind of listening I teach others to do. I think she is right about this one.

THE FOURTH KIND OF HEARING: LISTENING WITH AN UNDERSTANDING HEART

This is the way God wants all of us to listen. Jesus' parable leads to this obvious conclusion. We are to listen to God and especially to those we love with an understanding heart. Like the seed that fell on good and receptive soil that produced a bountiful harvest, this kind of listening is also productive. It produces the following five essential qualities of an interactive and harmonious marriage:

1. Gift love instead of need love. This kind of listening communicates a desire to give love without requiring any benefit in return. Remembering the words of Jesus, Luke writes in Acts 20:35, "It is more blessed to give than to receive."

2. Self-esteem. Letting the one talking know through your listening with an understanding heart affirms their value and worth to you. This strengthens their sense of importance and builds their self-confidence.
3. Mutual trust. This listening indicates a willingness to hear all the facts and details of an issue without rushing to judgment. Trust will be increased through experiencing patient listening. Proverbs 18:13, confirms this by saying, "If one gives answer before hearing, it is folly and shame." James 1:19, also says, "Let everyone be quick to listen, slow to speak."
4. Unselfishness. The union of marriage represents the attributes of God who made man and woman in His Image. God is generous, always giving and blessing, and never being selfish. A husband and wife are to listen with unselfish love in order to respond in the most appropriate ways to meet each other's highest needs. Philippians 2:3, teaches this so well; "Do nothing from selfish ambition or conceit, but in humility regard others as more important than yourself."
5. True understanding. Even when a husband or wife know almost everything there is to know about each other, and still loves and accepts you, there is no greater satisfaction a person can experience. This is what an understanding heart produces. The beautiful prayer of St. Francis of Assisi says it best, "Lord! Grant that I may seek more to understand than to be understood."

The value of listening with an understanding mind and a caring heart is powerfully illustrated in the story of Solomon becoming King of Israel. After King David finished his reign over Israel, his son Solomon was anointed King. I Kings 3: 5-14 records a dream he had while sleeping in Gibeon. God said, "Ask what I should give you." Solomon said, "Give your servant therefore an understanding mind to govern your people, able to discern between good and evil: for who can govern these, your great people?" God said to him, "Because you have asked this, and have not asked for yourself long life or riches or for the life of your enemies, but have asked for yourself understanding to discern what is right, I now do according to your word. Indeed, I give you a wise and discerning mind."

Solomon could have received anything in the world he desired for God promised to deliver whatever he wanted. Solomon knew what was most important and valuable. He asked and received from God, "A Discerning Mind and an Understanding Heart." Every couple as they begin the lifelong journey of marriage would be exceedingly wise to ask for the same: a discerning mind and understanding heart.

David Williams understood the value of this kind of mind and heart. In 1993, he was an outstanding professional football player. He was the starting tackle with the Houston Oilers Football Team. One evening when David and his wife were talking about the arrival of their first child in less than a month, he was listening with an understanding heart to her hopes and fears about having a baby. One of the things she said with tears in her eyes was, "When our baby is born, I want you to be in the delivery room with me. Your presence will give me strength and assurance that everything will be alright."

During the Sunday morning of the day when David was to play with his team in a very big game that would decide a playoff position, his wife excitedly said, "David, it is time. I feel the baby coming. We need to get to the hospital as quick as we can." David remembered his wife's request. He had heard her well, and his love would take precedent over all other matters.

On the way to the hospital, David called his coach. He told him the situation and apologized for having to miss the game. There was silence for one full minute. The coach pleaded with him to leave his wife at the hospital and get to the stadium as quickly as possible. David said, "No. The most important place for me today is by my wife's side. We will welcome our first child into our home together." The coach was furious. David missed the game and he paid a fine of $111,000. Their son, Scott, was born while the game was being played. He was healthy, big, and beautiful. David told reporters later that even if he had to pay a penalty of one million dollars, he would still have chosen to be with his wife.

David has an understanding heart. His wife has a husband who makes her feel like the most important woman in the world. Jesus says such a loving heart that listens with understanding produces a harvest that is thirty and sixty and a hundredfold.

CHAPTER SEVENTEEN

PEACE FOR ALL TIMES

Philippians 4: 4-7, *"Rejoice in the Lord always; again I say, Rejoice. Let all people know your gentleness for the Lord is with you. Have no anxiety about anything, but in everything by prayer and supplication with thanksgiving, let your requests be made known to God, and the PEACE of God which surpasses all understanding will keep your heart and mind in Christ Jesus."*

Each of us needs a plan for daily living. Every married couple needs a strategy to cope with life's situations in good and bad times. The scripture above directs us to the plan for PEACE. We all need this PEACE of God to maintain balance in our lives. It is equivalent to a ship's keel, which is the chief timber or synthetic beam extending on the bottom of a boat from bow to stern. Its function is to keep the vessel upright and to prevent it from turning over. Strong winds and turbulent waters can make it extremely uncomfortable for passengers and without a keel, a boat or ship will sometimes overturn. We can't control the weather or many circumstances of our lives. We <u>can</u>, however, make certain that we have a "keel for smoother sailing". The keel God provides for our balance is His PEACE.

This enables us to be prepared for the unexpected. An interesting story is told of a wife who kept her cool when confronted by a Game Warden one morning. After her husband returns to their lake cottage from several hours of fishing, she decides to get into his boat and leisurely drift on the water while reading a book. After enjoying the warm sun and peaceful solitude of the morning for about an hour, a Fish and Game

Warden pulls up beside her boat. He says, "Good morning, Ma'am. What are you doing?" "Reading a book," she replies as if it wasn't obvious. "You're in a restricted fishing area," he informs her. She calmly said to the officer, "I know you aren't allowed to fish in this part of the lake, and I'm not fishing. I am reading my book and enjoying this beautiful day."

He then rebukes her by saying, "Yes, but I see you have all the equipment. For all I know you could start at any moment. I'll have to take you to the court house and write you up." "If you do that, I'll have to charge you with sexual assault," the confident wife said in a very calm voice. Outraged the officer replied, "That's ridiculous. I haven't even touched you." "That's true, but you have all the equipment, and for all I know you could start at any moment," she answered.

As he pulled away from her boat astonished at her ability to counter his attempted arrest, he said with a smile, "Have a nice day, Ma'am."

This is a great example of having PEACE in heart, mind, and soul even during a difficult situation. One thing is sure. We all will have similar situations. Unjust confrontations, accidents, personal disappointments, crises, trials, and tribulations will threaten our tranquility and seek to sink our boat. How can we be prepared with a PEACE that will keep us stable and functioning at our best?

The answer comes from our faith connection with Jesus Christ. He alone gives us PEACE that will endure. When He was born, the Gospel of Luke announces, "A multitude of the heavenly host, praising God and saying, 'Glory to God in the highest heaven, and on earth PEACE, good will among people.'" Jesus is "The Prince of Peace" according to the Prophet Isaiah (9:6). As we abide in Jesus Christ and He abides in us, we have a PEACE that surpasses all understanding.

Wouldn't you like to be a person who experiences this PEACE which transcends and surpasses all other human emotions? Wouldn't you enjoy living with a person in marriage whose life was balanced with this PEACE? Jesus says in the Gospel of John 16: 33, "In Me, you may have PEACE." This PEACE does not come from the world or from what we can achieve or buy. Neither is it a PEACE that the forces of the world, governments, terrorists, or organizations can take from us. God's PEACE is for all times.

My most profound personal experience of the presence and power of this PEACE was in 1992. We were leading a group of Christians to Russia. Our first trip to the former Soviet Union was in January, 1990. Amazingly, we had a letter with special permission from Prime Minister Gorbechev of the communist government to deliver 3,000 Russian Bibles and Bible study manuals to citizens of Moscow, Leningrad, and Kiev. It was a frightening but marvelous mission trip. While in Moscow, we were able to assist a group of Russian Christians as they were starting a new Church called The Resurrection Christian Church.

Two years later, during our second trip, we were delivering $5,000 to the Pastor of this Moscow Church. When we crossed the border of Finland into Russia, our train was required to stop for inspection by the Russian authorities. Everyone on the train had to fill out a form indicating how much money was in their possession. There was an implied threat on the form that "severe penalties" would be imposed on anyone who was not honest. I therefore listed the $10,300 that I was carrying in my money belt around my waist. This included the $5,000 gift, $3,500 to pay gratuities during our trip, and $1,800 of my personal money. About twenty minutes after the cards were collected, Sandra, our daughter LeAnne, three friends and I were startled to hear a loud knock on our compartment door. When we opened it, two Russian soldiers asked for Jim Collins to come with them. They quickly said, "There is Big Problem. Wrong date on Visa. Come now!"

Reluctantly, I stood and went with them. Needless to say, there were many frightening thoughts that rushed through my mind like, "Will I ever see my wife, daughter, and friends again?" I was led off the train into the three story building next to the train loading dock. It was dimly lit. A Russian soldier was in front of me and one followed. As we walked down the narrow hallway, a man in a dress suit stepped out of a side room and took the lead as another one came behind the soldier following me. We then started up the stairs to the third floor. Sandra says I embellish the story every time I tell it to make it sound like a James Bond episode. But I am certain I saw scratches on the door facings and walls that looked to me like desperate escape attempts of other victims who had walked these halls before me.

As we approached the front office on the third floor, my heart was racing with fear. I felt the chill of stress and the uncertainty of what was about to happen. It was then that I silently cried out to the Lord, "Help me. Take charge of this situation, and ease my anxiety. Give me Your PEACE, O Lord, that will overrule this threat to my safety." I took several deep breaths and <u>felt</u> the Lord's Presence. I then said, "Let this be a witness to these Russians of Your Peace within me. Let them see strength greater than I possess. Protect me from harm, and give to these men a blessing they are not expecting."

Going into the room lighted by two open windows through which I could see the train below, a Russian Captain seated at the desk was pretending to talk with someone on the phone. Two other Russian soldiers were standing beside him. He said into the phone, "Big problem. Yes, we have big problem with wrong date on Visa. Yes, we will solve problem. Goodbye." He then looked at me, and asked, "Do you understand? Big problem. You solve."

I deliberately looked into the eyes of each of the five Russians in uniform and the two plain clothes men. I smiled with respect and confidence. I quietly said to the Lord, "Please let them see You in me. Give me Your PEACE that will remove all fear. Somehow help them understand that our group and I have come to their country to offer love and goodwill." It was obvious to me that I had been singled out from the other 250 passengers because probably I had declared the largest sum of money of any one on the train. It was money that they wanted. I then answered the Captain as politely and respectfully as I could by saying, "I realize this is a Big Problem. I am sorry that it is causing so much trouble. Please understand my group and I did not cause this problem. The Russian Embassy Office in America made the mistake." I did not blink or show any fear. I have never felt the Presence and PEACE of Jesus Christ more in my life than during this confrontation. It seemed that a spiritual line of communication and mutual respect opened between the Captain and me. I believe he saw in me what Philippians 4:4-7 makes possible: "Let all people know your gentleness for the Lord is with you. Have no anxiety about anything...and the PEACE of God which surpasses all understanding will keep your heart and mind in Christ Jesus."

Quite unexpectedly, he motioned to the two soldiers who had escorted me from the train for them to lead me back to my compartment. My heart began dancing within me as "I Rejoiced in The Lord" (Philippians 4:4). As we were boarding the train, the soldier behind me tapped me on the shoulder and said, "Gift." I turned and smiled. I took a twenty dollar bill from my billfold and gave it to him. I realized he had to take something back to the Captain to save face. He smiled and accepted it. He then said, "More gift." I gave him another twenty and said, "That's all the gifts."

After returning to Sandra, LeAnne, and our friends and shutting the compartment door, there was much laughter and celebration. They were greatly relieved to have me back, and I was so thankful to be out of that predicament. They were eager to hear every detail of my ordeal. It was hilarious as I recounted all that I saw, heard, and felt. I got more mileage from my exaggerated description than should have been allowed, but we had a lot of fun discussing it. Yet, it was clear to me that this experience fulfilled Jesus' promise to be with us and give us "A PEACE For All Times." It was proof positive His PEACE works even during such a horrific hour.

In the following eight days, our group enjoyed wonderful sights, museums, Churches, and visits with many Russian children and adults. We had gifts and Bibles in their language to share with them. We especially were blessed in the worship services with our "Sister Congregation" of The Resurrection Church. They were pleased to receive the $5,000 gift from the Peachtree Christian Church, Atlanta, Georgia. When we returned by train to the Finland border station, there was another knock on our compartment door. The same Russian soldier who took me off the train opened the door! With a huge grin he said, "Old Friends." We shook hands, and laughed together.

This PEACE that was the highlight of my trip to Russia in 1992 can be ours every day on our journey of marriage. Sandra and I have memorized Philippians 4:4-7, and we often say it individually and as a couple. These few verses contain more superlative words than any other short passage in the entire Bible. Some of these are: "Rejoice always," "everyone," "anything," "everything," and "surpasses all understanding." A superlative word is used when something supersedes all others. This is therefore the nature of God's superlative gifts He wants us to have in Jesus Christ. There are seven of them listed in this superlative scripture:

1. **REJOICING** instead of despairing. We are to rejoice in the Lord always because He has already done so much for us. He has forgiven our sins, assured us of Eternal Life, promised to be with us always, and given us Grace, Love, Peace, Joy, and Hope. Even if He never does anything more for us, He has already blessed us for all Eternity. We, therefore, are to Rejoice always. When we do, the negatives of life are changed into positives. Attitudes are improved. We are more fun to be with when there is rejoicing in our hearts.

2. **GENTLENESS** instead of anger. It is easy to let frustration, stress, and disappointment ignite bursts of anger. This usually causes us to say and do things we later regret. It also makes people around us feel uncomfortable, tense, and distant because they don't want to provoke another time of conflict. We can be strong and true to our convictions without anger. We need the gift of gentleness to think and act wisely, and to treat others with consideration.

3. **HIS PRESENCE** instead of loneliness. Philippians 4:5, assures us by trusting the Lord, rejoicing in the Lord, and being gentle He is

with us. We are never alone. We should practice gentleness so we do not embarrass our Lord by saying and doing things from anger. It is a proven fact, "Anger does not produce God's righteousness" (James 1:20).

4. **CONFIDENCE** instead of anxiety. Our Lord asks us to trust Him with future matters and strive to do the best we can one day at a time. He says in The Sermon On The Mount, Matthew 6: 25 – 34, "Do not worry about your life, what you will eat or what you will drink, or about your body, what you will wear...Do not be anxious about tomorrow for tomorrow will be anxious for itself...But as for you, seek first God's Kingdom and His righteousness, and all things you need will be given to you." Philippians 4: 6, "Have no anxiety about anything," confirms our Lord's teaching.

5. **PRAYER** instead of doubt. Since the Lord is with us always, we are to be aware of His Presence, and talk to Him without ceasing as II Thessalonians 5:16 encourages us to do. Just a few years ago, who could have imagined that cell phones would connect us to almost any person anywhere in the world? But far greater than this technological achievement is God's gift of Prayer by which we can talk with Him always.

6. **THANKSGIVING** instead of complaining. God has blessed us with life and His Love and Goodness. Having a thankful heart is also a gift. The attitude of gratitude enables us to realize how fortunate we are in all circumstances. The Apostle Paul says in Philippians 4: 11, "I have learned to be content with whatever I have." He is the one who says, "Rejoice in the Lord Always, and give Thanks." There is nothing that endears us more to others, especially in marriage, than appreciation. This is even truer with God. The more thankful we are for His many blessings, the more He wants to give us. If we are not thankful for what He has already done, why should He do more for us?

7. **PEACE** instead of confusion. Without PEACE, we often are disoriented and frantic to make things right. With PEACE we can function at our best. We can better control our feelings and emotions as we think and act responsibly. This gift of PEACE surpasses all understanding. It guards our heart and mind in Christ Jesus so we are not confused. This is why millions of people can be comforted with "The Serenity Prayer" which talks about God's superlative gift of "Peace For All Times." It says:

God grant me the serenity
To accept the things I cannot change;
Courage to change the things I can;
And wisdom to know the difference.
Living one day at a time;
Enjoying one moment at a time;
Accepting hardships as the pathway to peace...
Trusting that He will make all things right
If I surrender to His Will;
That I may be reasonably happy in this life
And supremely happy with Him
Forever in the next. Amen.

Reinhold Niebuhr (1892 – 1971)

CHAPTER EIGHTEEN

LET'S T.A.L.K.

Romans 12: 9-12, *"Let love be genuine; hate what is evil, hold fast to what is good; love one another with mutual affection; outdo one another in showing honor. Do not lag in zeal, be ardent in spirit, serve the Lord. Rejoice in hope, be patient in suffering, persevere in prayer."*

This scripture from Paul's letter to the Christians in Rome is excellent counsel for a Christian marriage. It gives the characteristics of a healthy and dynamic marriage that maintain good communication, mutual affection, togetherness, and kindness. Notice the emphasis on genuine love, avoiding what is wrong and embracing what is good, seeking to outdo one another by cherishing and honoring each other, and praying to the Lord for enthusiasm, hope, and patience. It provides husbands and wives a guide for ongoing dialogue that is more interactive than just speaking and hearing words.

A husband was amused as he read an article about the number of words men and women speak each day. He said to his wife, "This confirms what I have always suspected. Women talk twice as much as men. This article indicates that women say about 30,000 words each day compared to men, who only need to use 15,000 words. Why do you think women talk so much?" His wife replied without even looking up, "The answer is obvious to any woman who is married. A wife has to repeat everything she says before her husband hears her." Her husband looked up from the paper he was reading and asked, "What was that you said?"

Words are important, but meaningful communication in marriage does not result from the number of words spoken. Even if many words are frequently spoken, a marriage will starve to death if husbands and wives do not make four essential investments in their relationship. I believe they constitute the essence of real T.A.L.K. that provides nourishment for a lasting and loving marriage. I have found in my marriage and through the many counseling sessions I have experienced with married couples that these four elements of T.A.L.K. are:

T - TOGETHERNESS
A - APPRECIATION
L - LAUGHTER
K - KINDNESS

Consider first, the "T" in T.A.L.K. It stands for **TOGETHERNESS**. There are times in every marriage when a husband or wife becomes frustrated during a conversation because one is not emotionally present. They are in the same room, but they aren't together. Words are being spoken and information is being exchanged, but communication is not taking place. Togetherness is absent.

This has been one of my shortcomings with Sandra. Many times she has stopped our conversation by observing I was being distracted. I was not listening with both ears. I was not fully comprehending what she was sharing with me. It was not intentional. I would never want her to think I was disinterested. Yet, I was not participating in the discussion as I should. It is easy for each of us to be too tired, too busy, too distracted, and too preoccupied with planning our response that we are not emotionally involved in the conversation. I have therefore, learned that just as I want Sandra to be really present when I am talking to her, I need to make a deliberate effort to be present in our "togetherness" when she is having a conversation with me.

Some of the ways I try to practice "togetherness" with Sandra when we are talking are: (1) establish good eye contact and body language by turning toward her; (2) wait for my turn to speak without interrupting her when she is talking; (3) eliminate distractions to make it clear she is more important than the computer, TV, cell phone, and reading materials; (4) remember from the New Testament James 1:19, "Be quick to listen, slow to speak, slow to anger" since anger usually produces more anger; (5) avoid becoming defensive or over personalizing an issue when specific concerns are being discussed; (6) be aware of the non-verbal messages that come from voice tones, shrugging the shoulders, a quivering chin, crossing arms, stepping back, reaching out, smiles, frowns, tears, rolling eyes, and sighing; (7) listen actively with good feedback techniques like "I hear what you are saying," "Do you really feel that way?", "Tell me more about that," and "Help me understand how you came to that decision"; (8) wait to be asked before giving advice; and (9) reach for her hand when loving support would be affirmed.

Although these are disciplines which have improved my togetherness with Sandra, they are basic principles that can be helpful to both husbands and wives who want to experience real T.A.L.K. It is also important to develop "togetherness" as a daily priority so it will be felt when conversation actually takes place.

Some of the ways we can do this are: (1) prove in word and action that you are best friends and really enjoy being with each other; (2) share spiritual opportunities of worshipping and praying together, reading a devotional booklet each day, and studying the Bible in an orderly way; (3) exercise together; (4) work as a team to accomplish house and yard projects; (5) volunteer as husband and wife in a community service program; (6) play together in entertainment venues of mutual enjoyment, and (7) plan specific times and places to be sexually intimate.

These patterns for married life become the foundation on which meaningful conversation can occur. The "Togetherness Factor" will be clearly established, and T.A.L.K. will be a natural and satisfying dialogue.

"A" is the second letter of T.A.L.K. It represents **APPRECIATION**. It is a vital component of maintaining open and responsive communication in marriage. When a husband and wife give each other assurance of being appreciated, their talk is more spontaneous, respectful, and honest than when they feel they are being taken for granted.

Many surveys have verified this to be true. For example, twenty two married couples at a retreat in Kansas City were asked to rate the importance of financial security, freedom from stress, appreciation, forgiveness, honesty, times of recreation, and intimate sex relations. It was first agreed by all couples that each of the qualities listed were very important. But when the leader insisted on everyone identifying the one most important quality, thirty nine of the forty four people there named appreciation. The one thing they said was needed most in marriage to sustain enjoyable communication was the assurance from their spouse that their efforts and contributions were not being ignored. It was appreciation, they said, that motivated them to do their best and to maintain a positive attitude even when disappointments and problems were being discussed.

I can identify with their rating appreciation as the most important factor. Throughout my young life and during the fifty years of my Christian ministry, I have been conscious of the joy of appreciation. Receiving appreciation has been and still is the primary goal of all my endeavors. It is not approval, but a positive response from others who have been blessed in some way by my services. When a Church search committee interviewed me for their Senior Pastor position some years ago, one of the members asked, "What is your greatest motivation for self-discipline in performing your duties as a pastor?" I responded without a moment of hesitation, "It is being appreciated." I explained that I did not seek everyone's approval or agreement with my views and goals. But I very much needed and wanted the appreciation from those I serve who simply realize I am trying to do my best for them and for the Glory of God.

This has been especially true in our marriage. Nothing warms my heart more than when Sandra expresses appreciation for me as her husband, and for the things I do to please her. She also loves for me to leave notes from time to time indicating my gratitude for her and for the many extra things she does for me. As I indicated in Chapter Ten while discussing our "G.R.O.W. Prayer," her words of thanksgiving to God for me is a thrilling and humbling gift every time I hear her say, "I am grateful for Jim and his love." I hope that after I die, Sandra will at least consider doing what a Southern mountain woman had chiseled in her husband's tombstone. The epitaph said, "He always appreciated me."

We certainly don't want to deprive our marriage of appreciation as the farmer in Vermont apparently did for forty years. As he and his wife were sitting on the front steps one evening, he spoke up and said, "Honey, you've been such a wonderful wife to me through the years of our living and working together, there are times I can hardly keep from telling you how much I appreciate you."

We can only ask, "Why not? Why not express appreciation often and perhaps every day?" If we want to keep our talk alive and satisfying, appreciation is the key. Without appreciation communication dwindles, and marriage becomes complacent. A husband or wife who begins to realize they are just expected to be faithful, dutiful, and available whenever needed without any sign of appreciation sooner or later will ask, "Why should I even try?" But when appreciation is communicated with words and deeds, there is no limit of one's desire to give and to do his or her best to keep marriage vibrant and happy.

The third letter of T.A.L.K. is "L". It stands for **LAUGHTER**. It is the delightful flavor in talking together as husband and wife. It is the rainbow that gives color to good communication. One night several years ago, a frantic wife called for me to come help her. Her husband had just died from a heart attack on the kitchen floor. I got there as soon as I could and before the EMC personnel arrived. As her Pastor, I comforted her, and shared her shock and grief. I also shared our faith in Jesus Christ who is the Resurrection and the Life and our assurance of Eternal Life. As a couple, they did not have children, but they enjoyed several animals in their home that were a part of their family. But the one thing I will always remember her saying as we waited for the ambulance to come was, "He always made me laugh. He was so much fun to live with. We always had something to talk about and many things to laugh about." Many couples refer to each other as "soul mates." She would say, "We were laugh mates."

In the Bible, Proverbs 17:22, says, "A cheerful heart is a good medicine, but a downcast spirit dries up the bones." Medical science confirms this about laughter. It boosts the immune system, reduces stress, relaxes the muscles, and is an excellent exercise for the internal organs of the body. It even helps us sleep better when we can laugh or share a humorous experience before saying good night. Married couples who are content with each other laugh a lot. They enjoy sharing with each other the funny things that occurred in the course of their day. They can poke good natured fun at each other and laugh at themselves. They can even see the humor in many of life's stressful moments. Laughter, therefore, keeps us from taking ourselves too seriously.

I remember early in our marriage Sandra and I were sitting in the dark watching a slide show about the hungry people in Africa during a Wednesday night Church fellowship dinner. It was a very serious occasion. Everyone had been given a "Sugar Daddy Sucker" to remind us of the song, "He's Got the Whole World in His Hands." It was very sticky. All of a sudden the sucker stuck to the cap on my front tooth, and pulled it off. During our childhood, my brother had accidently knocked my tooth out while we were playing with wooden rifles. There was enough light from the slide projector in the fellowship hall for Sandra to see this open space in my teeth. She never knew that one of my front teeth was just a cap. She could not contain herself. She began to laugh amidst the serious program we were watching.

My expectation was for her to give me some sympathy. Here I was, the Pastor of the Church, with members of the congregation hearing this commotion. Sandra was laughing. She spontaneously said out loud, "His tooth fell out." Others began to laugh. Then all of a sudden my humiliation became funny to me. We all laughed and enjoyed a little good medicine. Somehow, because of laughter, every one there was in a more willing mood to give generously to the Week of Compassion Fund for the hungry people in Africa! Sandra and I have laughed many times during the years at the mere mention of this experience.

Laughter in marriage builds good will and enables husbands and wives to talk more freely with each other. It makes them feel closer. Being light hearted reduces the serious mood of difficult issues. Laughing at your own mistakes communicates awareness that you are not always right. It makes you more vulnerable to each other and encourages greater acceptance of each other's imperfections. It also enables you to be playful and not take life so seriously.

This was one of the first great differences in my life that I experienced soon after Sandra and I married. The first twenty nine years of my life would be described correctly as good natured, but serious. I had always been the achiever, the doer, and many times the leader. But after receiving the gift of marriage, I discovered a dimension of life that increased my fun of living. I somehow felt complete with Sandra, and my joy seemed to overflow. I laughed more in the first year of our marriage than ever before. I was more silly and playful than I had ever been. For example I noticed one evening as I was brushing my teeth that Sandra was standing at the bathroom door watching what I was doing. I then pretended to take out dentures and wash them in the sink. She couldn't see exactly what I was doing, but she got the impression that I wore false teeth. She rushed in to confront me with the deception of marrying her without full disclosure. When I convinced her that I was only pretending, we both burst out with laughter. There is no greater affirmation of love and enjoyment than when a husband and wife laugh together.

Another playful time with Sandra was when one of my silly acts produced much laughter, at least for me. She claimed it was grounds for divorce. It was the day Sandra and I went to my brother's lake in Douglasville, Georgia. I wanted to fish and she wanted to gather some vegetables from the garden. When I turned the boat over on the bank before I pushed it onto the water, I saw the biggest jumping frog of my life. I reached down and quickly grabbed it by the legs. It stretched out to be about twenty inches long. I emptied some fishing lures from a paper sack and put the frog inside. I got into the boat and called for Sandra. When she came near to where I was fishing, I asked her to pick up the paper bag and "reach inside." She saw it move, and I almost fell out of the boat with laughter! She turned white with fear and didn't think it was very funny. I pulled the boat in and as I was retrieving the frog from the bag inch by inch, Sandra jumped into the boat. I could not contain myself from hysterical laughter. It was only after I let the frog go and comforted Sandra that she could laugh with me. The episode has grown funnier through the years, but at the time my exercise of humor almost caused me to croak.

It feels good to laugh together. It's one thing we can do that never gets boring. The more we learn each other's "laugh buttons," the more fun it is to live together. Our humor should always be good natured and never used to make fun of each other. Laughter alone will not cure severe marital ills, nor make addictions, abuse, or irresponsible acts acceptable. But laughter does help us get through many of the difficult times of life. It strengthens our relationship in marriage and helps us talk about the important issues of home life without allowing them to feel so heavy.

"K" is the last letter of T.A.L.K. It represents **KINDNESS** which many regard as the most important factor in good communication. Some of the characteristics of kindness are described in Romans 12: 9-12, which is the scripture at the beginning of this chapter. They are mutual affection, showing honor, controlling anger, practicing patience, doing what is good, and avoiding harm to others.

Kindness is one of the attributes of God. In Titus 3: 4-5, it is written, "When the goodness and loving kindness of God our Savior appeared, He saved us, not because of any works of righteousness that we had done, but according to His mercy." We, therefore, according to Colossians 3:12, "as God's chosen ones" are to clothe ourselves with compassion and kindness. The fruit of the Holy Spirit in Galatians 5: 22 is "Kindness." A Christian woman filled with the Holy Spirit is mentioned in The Book of Acts 9:36, with these words, "Now in Joppa there was a disciple named Tabitha, which in Greek is Dorcas. She was devoted to kindness and acts of charity."

Kindness is one of God's gifts that has great value in growing a relationship of affection. It can be the network for a husband and wife to share their hopes and dreams, their thoughts and concerns, their hurts and struggles, their appreciations and affirmations, and their joys and laughter for a life time. Kindness is often the attraction during courtship that leads to marriage. It is therefore assumed that kindness will be received and given throughout marriage. When it isn't, almost everything else that is good comes apart. Without kindness many hurtful things are said that could have been avoided. Many positive acts are neglected causing the foundation of marriage to erode.

It should be obvious then for a healthy marriage to be nurtured, "random acts of kindness" are needed every day. Let me suggest the following as a startup list for husbands and wives:

1. Greet each other every morning with a smile and wishes for a happy day.
2. Ask if there is any special task you can do for your mate today.
3. Listen and comfort each other if there is a problem.
4. Think "kindness" before you speak and delete negative comments.
5. Leave a note for your mate to find with a word of love and encouragement.
6. Call your mate during the day, or send an e-mail to say, "I'm thinking about you."
7. Express appreciation for acts of kindness your mate recently did for you.
8. Go grocery shopping together and share the planning of meals and menus.
9. Invite your mate to exercise with you or enable your mate to exercise alone.
10. Maintain habits of neatness and practice good hygiene for cleanliness and heath.
11. Pray for your spouse and often ask if there are special requests you need to know about.
12. Plan a night out each week and occasionally a weekend trip you both can enjoy.

Kindness is contagious. As you live by the Golden Rule to do unto others as you would want them to do unto you, you are creating goodwill and cooperation. Your mate will be more willing to show kindness to you if you show kindness. No one is kind all the time, but when we make kindness a priority with our spouse, you can be sure more kindness will be given to you. Kindness is appreciated and remembered. Each act of kindness creates a "relationship credit." These credits are stored in one's memory like dollars are saved in a bank. These credits for kindness will be returned to you for they grow in value. The more credits you have stored up in your mate's memory, the easier it is to overcome mistakes and times of frustrations. There are no substitutes for kindness. It cannot be replaced with gifts, money, exotic trips, or flattering words. Kindness has its own unique value and rewards. Someone has said, "You can't give it away. The more kindness you show to your mate, the more kindness will return to you."

This is also true with strangers, neighbors, and friends. Your mate will grow in respect for you as you show kindness to others. Sandra has always excelled with this quality of her character. She constantly amazes me with her smile toward others, and her ability to say something nice to employees at the various stores in which we shop. She can change a person's sour disposition with the twinkle of her eye, because she is so kind to others and to me. She gives me some credit for this although she has mastered the art of kindness more than I have. I taught her what a professor in my Theology School taught me as I was studying for the Christian ministry. He quoted a German Pastor, Martin Niemoeller, during the World War II era who said, "Be kind to everyone you meet, for everyone is carrying a heavy burden and fighting a difficult battle." He expanded a comment Plato had made and influenced millions of people with his words.

Regardless of who gets credit for words that encourage kindness, acts of kindness are profoundly important in developing community both in marriage and with friends. Positive talking is stimulated when a person hears words of kindness and sees acts of thoughtfulness. Everyone benefits from simple and random acts of kindness, especially husbands and wives.

These four essentials of good T.A.L.K., **TOGETHERNESS, APPRECIATION, LAUGHTER,** and **KINDNESS,** are like four sections of a sturdy bridge that keep a husband and wife connected. When you say to your mate, "We need to T.A.L.K.," make sure you remember what it really should be. An anonymous poet obviously experienced marriage for many years before he could write the following words. I believe they capture the essence of what T.A.L.K. is all about:

A Bridge

They say a wife and husband, bit by bit
Can rear between their lives a mighty wall.
So thick they cannot speak with
ease through it,
Nor can they see across, it stands so tall.
Its nearness frightens them, but each alone
Is powerless to tear its bulk away;
And each, heartbroken, wishes he had known
For such a wall the magic word to say.

So let us build with master art, my dear,
A bridge of faith between your life and mine –
A bridge of tenderness and very near –

A bridge of understanding, strong and fine;
Until we have built so many lovely ties,
There never will be room for walls to rise.

CHAPTER NINETEEN

THE UNFORGETTABLE WEDDING

John 2: 1-11, *"On the third day there was a wedding in Cana of Galilee, and the mother of Jesus was there. Jesus and his disciples had also been invited to the wedding. When the wine gave out, the mother of Jesus said to Him, 'They have no wine.' And Jesus said to her, 'Woman, what concern is that to you and to Me? My hour has not yet come.' His mother said to the servants, 'Do whatever He tells you.' Now standing there were six stone water jars for the Jewish rites of purification, each holding twenty or thirty gallons. Jesus said to them, 'Fill the jars with water.' And they filled them up to the brim. He said to them, 'Now draw some out, and take it to the chief steward.' So they took it. When the steward tasted the water that had become wine, and did not know where it came from (though the servants who had drawn the water knew), the steward called the bridegroom and said to him, "Everyone serves the good wine first, and then the inferior wine after the guests have become drunk. But you have kept the good wine until now.' Jesus did this, the first of his signs (miracles), in Cana of Galilee, and revealed His Glory; and His disciples believed in Him."*

I have performed many weddings through the years that are unforgettable. One of these was for a delightful couple that I enjoyed meeting with during premarital counseling sessions. The groom was a very large African-American football player who was an outstanding guard for the University of Georgia. He wanted to prepare me before everyone came to the rehearsal. He said all of his groomsmen from different parts of the country played football with him in college. Each of them, he explained, weighs more than 250 pounds. The chancel of our sanctuary at the

Peachtree Christian Church in Atlanta is spacious, but it could hardly contain nine such large men plus the groom and me.

When I went to meet with the groom and the groomsmen about fifteen minutes before the wedding, I went into panic mode when the best man told me his tuxedo did not arrive with the others. He was standing in a pair of shorts, flip flops, and a not too clean T shirt. He asked if it would be OK for him to go out and stand with the groom dressed as he was. I said, "Absolutely NOT."

In desperation, a solution quickly can to my mind. I asked him if he was active in a Church. He said he was a deacon. Without explaining, I hurried to my study and returned with a black robe that belonged to our former pastor, Dr. Robert Burns, who was larger than I was. I told the best man, "This is what we are going to do. You will wear this robe, and later in the ceremony I will call on you as a deacon to give a short prayer. Everyone then will understand why you are the only groomsman wearing a black robe similar to the one I am wearing. " His face flushed, but he didn't argue with me. The organist began to play the wedding processional, and the men and I marched out to the chancel with smiles on our faces. Sure enough, when the time came, the deacon of the hour stepped forward and gave a beautiful prayer. No one was the wiser except the few who noticed flip flops under the robe.

As unusual as this wedding was, it could not compare with "The Most Unforgettable Wedding" of all time. There has never been a wedding like the one Jesus attended in Cana of Galilee. It is described in the Gospel of John Chapter 2. Our Lord was there to redeem the first gift God presented to man and woman at the time of Creation. Jesus blessed the marriage of this husband and wife as a clear proclamation of God's original purpose for man and woman. Marriage is a sacred union given of God, and Jesus' Presence at that wedding affirmed the eternal value of this Covenant. This was the perfect setting for Jesus to perform His first miracle of His earthly mission. He came to restore through His ministry of teaching and by His death and resurrection, the righteousness of each person through his or her genuine faith in God. He began this redemptive work at a wedding. His first of seven miracles, according to the Gospel of John, had a profound message for the world regarding marriage. He turned the water in the six large stone urns into wine. These urns would hold twenty to thirty gallons of water that were used for Jewish purification rites. Jesus miraculously converted the 150 or more gallons of water into the best wine that has ever been on earth. And it all happened at a wedding. What was the purpose of this mighty act?

In all my Biblical and Theological studies, I never understood why our Lord did this! Several years ago, when Sandra and I led another group of Christians to the Holy Land, we visited the beautiful Church built on the site of this Wedding in Galilee. As we prepared for a time of worship in the sanctuary during which time we lead all the married couples in the renewing of their marriage vows, the Senior Priest invited me to go with him into the sacristy. He presented me with his white robe that he wanted me to wear during the service.

After the priest left me alone, I began preparing Holy Communion for our worship service. I had no idea I was about to experience one of the most blessed moments of my entire life. As I was pouring the wine into a Chalice that I had bought for the occasion, I had the <u>strongest</u> sense of our Lord's Presence. It had never occurred to me before, but I had a burning desire to know why Jesus chose wine as his first miracle. He had all power and authority in heaven and on earth to do anything He decided to do. Why the wine? I asked the Lord to give me some understanding of the message He was demonstrating for the couple married at this wedding some two thousand years ago. It was an unplanned and surprising experience for me to ask Jesus Christ, "Just what is the meaning of Your first miracle when You turned the water into wine?" Humbly and expectantly I asked Him, "Teach me the intent of Your Heart and the message You wanted all people to know about the importance of marriage."

Immediately there came to me a flash of insight unlike any other time of inspiration that I have ever known. Jesus made known to me, simply because I asked Him in faith believing He would answer, three reasons and profound lessons from His water to wine miracle. I was able to go into the sanctuary where our group was quietly waiting with the message that had been given to me. I was filled with joy! I was eager to share with them what I had just learned.

I placed the Chalice of wine and a loaf of bread on the altar and read the story of the wedding that occurred in Cana. Then I told them the following three lessons our Lord's miracle gives to us about marriage.

The First: "Wine Represents Purity"

Water is not always safe to drink. In our travels to certain countries over the years, our guides were adamant about not drinking the native water. They insisted on our drinking only bottled water that was certified as pure and clean. Wine, however, that is properly prepared is safe to drink. It is pure and uncontaminated.

Jesus' gift of wine to the newly married couple reveals God's desire for purity in marriage. Hebrews 13:4 clearly states, "Let marriage be held in honor by all, and let the marriage bed be kept undefiled; for God will judge fornicators and adulterers." During a Christian wedding ceremony, a man and woman promise to be faithful to each other by forsaking all others. They make a vow to keep themselves pure from sexual sin and give their bodies only to each other. God wants us to have marriages that are successful and filled with love, joy, peace, and a clear conscience. His plan works when we remain true to our promises of faithfulness and allow God's blessings to be upon our marriage.

Sexual impurity has five devastating results on marriage. First, it destroys love relationships with God and with one's mate. Second, it is the number one cause of divorce. Third, it creates guilt even when it is kept a secret. Fourth, it increases the chance of sexually transmitted diseases. Fifth, it can lead to financial devastation. Even though some parts of the entertainment world and the musical industry glamorize sexual immorality, the ultimate consequences are dehumanizing. Theirs is a prescription that leads to unhappiness. Just maybe, God's plan for purity before and after the wedding is for our highest good. I am convinced it is.

The lure of immoral sex is continually present in our world today. We are sexual beings and are easily tempted to allow pornography or lust to misuse God's gift. The Holy Spirit gives us power to both resolve and maintain purity in matters of sexual enjoyment. Sex is God's gift, and it brings great pleasure to a man and woman when they commit themselves to sexual purity in marriage.

The Second: "Wine Represents Joy"

There is nothing that adds more joy to a happy occasion than a glass of good wine. Jesus added joy to this "Unforgettable Wedding" by turning the urns of water into wine. The best and most valuable wine that has ever been on this earth was the wine Jesus created that day in Cana of Galilee. Wouldn't you love to have just a sip of it? Can you even imagine the heavenly taste and aroma of this fruit of the vine? It was so wonderful, the steward, according to John 2:10, called the bridegroom and said to him, "Everyone serves the good wine first, and then the inferior wine...But you have kept the good wine until now." Obviously he and all who tasted the wine Jesus presented had never experienced anything so delicious. There was increased joy at that happy wedding because Jesus was present with them providing unforgettable wine.

141

Whether a married couple drinks wine or not, Jesus wants joy to be in their lives every day. Joy is defined as the presence of ecstatic happiness, pleasure, and satisfaction. It is the grateful awareness of the presence of God's blessings even when other circumstances in life may be difficult. Jesus says in John 15: 9 - 11, "As the Father has loved me, so I have loved you; abide in my love...I have said these things to you so that my joy may be in you, and that your joy may be complete." His joy is a gift that the world cannot give nor take away. It is sweeter than fine wine.

This joy is promised to a husband and wife who have a personal relationship with Jesus Christ. Jesus explained that we can abide in Him and He in us just like the branches abide in the vine in a grape vineyard. He says, "I am the vine, you are the branches. Those who abide in me and I in them bear much fruit" (John 15: 5-6)." In Jesus Christ our mistakes and sins are forgiven. We have peace with God and with ourselves which opens the way for true joy. Paul says in Romans 5: 1 "Therefore, since we are justified by faith, we have peace with God through our Lord Jesus Christ, through whom we have obtained access to this grace in which we stand; and we boast in our hope of sharing the glory of God."

When Jesus is present in our hearts and in our homes, we can "Rejoice in the Lord always." Even if He never does anything else for us, He has already given us God's Love, Grace, Forgiveness, Hope, and Power through His Holy Spirit, and Eternal Life. Therefore, in the best of times and in the worst of times, we can "Rejoice in the Lord always." Jesus Christ is the source of heartfelt and lasting joy. Just as wine represents joy, as long as we don't drink too much, our Lord and Savior blesses marriage with the joy of His Presence. If God be for us then who can be against us? (Romans 8: 31)

The Third: "Wine Represents Partnership"

Wine does not flow naturally from a spring or a stream of water. Wine is the result of partnership. Jesus wanted to encourage couples who marry to enter into a living partnership, instead of relying upon themselves only for the success of their marriage.

Wine is the culmination of a process. It takes people planting a vineyard in the good earth that God has created. God sends the rains and the sunshine to nurture and grow the vineyard. People prune the vines and branches to increase their productivity. They work with nature in cultivating the grapes as the clusters ripen for harvest. Then the people, with strength and wisdom provided by God, gather the grapes, extract the juice, and patiently wait for nature to bring about fermentation. Then they bottle the wine for consumption.

Marriage is also a mysterious and marvelous partnership. It involves a husband and a wife, the wonder of nature, and the God of our creation who provides the Love, Truth, and Power needed for a growing and joy filled union. Born from this oneness are blessings for family members, friends, neighbors, and community. Children are the fruit of marriage who make a home complete.

When we are growing up, we often tell our parents and our teachers, "Let me do it now." This is a healthy part of our learning to be responsible and discovering our talents and abilities. But when we mature and become adults, as Paul says in I Corinthians 13: 11, "I put an end to childish ways." I believe he means we humble ourselves and become less selfish. We accept help from others, and we willingly serve others as we have the opportunity. Instead of childish independence, we learn to be interdependent. We value and welcome partnership. We humble ourselves to God and seek to be obedient to His Will in all the areas of our lives. We commit ourselves to the one we marry with devotion, faithfulness, and sharing the daily routines and rhythms of life. In other words, we accept the process of partnering with our best friend and lover, with God who holds the gifts of marriage, and with nature that guides us through the stages of maturity. Marriage, as it was intended to be, is a partnership. It is about us, and we, and our. Together we become living stones in the foundation of our Church, places of work, community, nation, and world. Jesus teaches us these principles in His unprecedented miracle of turning water into wine.

This "Unforgettable Wedding" in Cana of Galilee will always remind us of God's plan for marriage. Just as there will "Always Be A Wedding" as long as humanity lives on earth, so there will be successful and happy marriages for couples who are wise enough to follow God's plan of PURITY, JOY, and PARTNERSHIP.

CHAPTER TWENTY

BE FRUITFUL AND MULTIPLY

Genesis 2:27 – 28, *"In the image of God He created them; male and female He created them. God blessed them, and God said to them, 'Be fruitful and multiply, and fill the earth.'"*

E very person born of woman is precious unto the Lord. Each of us is created in the "Image of God." We reflect God's very nature. When a man and woman join together in marriage, they become more like God. The two become one, and together as one flesh in their marital union, they represent the Oneness of God. When they are fruitful and have a child, their family is extended to magnify other attributes of God. The father heart of God and the mother heart of God are experienced in the sacred act of creating new life. More than any other place, the fullness of God is manifested in every home that honors and loves God.

One husband and wife who had been married for several years wanted this experience of being parents, but they were not successful in having children. They, therefore, devoted themselves to their work. Since they both were spending so much time in developing their careers, they decided to hire a live-in maid. A lovely young woman took the job which included cooking all the meals and doing the basic housework. She was doing a fine job, and her polite personality was very pleasing to the couple.

However, after several months in their home she submitted her resignation. The couple was shocked and disappointed. "Why are you leaving us?" they asked. She hesitated, but finally said, "I met this good looking man on my day off, and we developed a relationship. Now I am pregnant."

The wife said, "Look, we don't want to lose you. My husband and I have been wanting a child. If you will stay as our maid, we will adopt your baby." She looked at her husband, and he nodded in agreement. The maid said this would be fine with her. The baby came, the adoption papers were signed and everyone was happy.

Things went well until six months later. The maid announced that she was pregnant again. She offered to resign, but the couple said, "Please don't leave us. We will adopt your second baby as we did the first one." The maid agreed. The second baby was adopted, and life continued in the home as usual. That is until a few months later, the maid said she would have to leave. Same thing. She was pregnant. The couple made the adoption offer again, and the maid agreed to continue working as their cook and housekeeper.

Three months after the third baby was adopted, the maid met with the couple and said, "I am definitely leaving this time!" "Don't tell me you're pregnant again," exclaimed the lady of the house.

"No," she said. "'I'm leaving because there are just too many kids in this house to pick up after!'"

This maid certainly did not have children in the way God intended. However, she was right in discovering that children require a lot of hard work and a great deal of patience. What she failed to realize was that children are an awesome blessing and a heritage from the Lord.

God's purpose for marriage is not primarily for couples to have children. Marriage is the means of fulfillment for a man and woman. Children are not a necessity for a happy marriage, nor for God's purpose of marriage to be accomplished. But truly children are a marvelous gift to a husband and wife just as we were to our parents whether they admit it or not. Our two daughters have enhanced our marriage and home more than any other experience, achievement, or possession ever could. Although there have been many difficulties, challenges, and struggles that come with children, the joy of our daughters, Leslie and LeAnne, is our greatest gift next to our marriage and salvation in Jesus Christ.

There are many in our society who do not regard children as gifts from God. This is well-evidenced by the astounding number of abortions that occur every year in America. There is also a widespread judgment that children are a bother, a threat to one's personal goals, an obstacle to individual success and enjoyment of life, and an expense that needs to be avoided. Thank God these attitudes did not prevent our parents from giving us the opportunity to live. Yet it is true, children require great sacrifices from mothers and fathers. Raising them successfully is perhaps the greatest challenge we face in life. Someone has said, "Our children are born savages. Our job is to civilize them." I guess that was said of us as well. Even Socrates, 426 years before the birth of Jesus Christ said, "Children today are tyrants. They contradict their parents, they gobble their food, and they terrorize their teachers." If he were speaking about the immoral, disrespectful, and rebellious conditions which surround young people today, I can only imagine what his commentary would sound like.

It is, therefore, increasingly important for Christian couples to mature in marriage and establish Godly standards for their home before they have their first child. This is not always possible, but in all circumstances of marriage, wise husbands and wives will seek God's guidance in laying the right foundation on which a child can grow responsibly. Psalm 127 speaks this truth in these words, "Unless the Lord builds the house, those who build it labor in vain...children are indeed a heritage from the Lord, the fruit of the womb, a reward." Psalm 128 continues this teaching by saying, "Happy is everyone who fears the Lord, who walks in His ways. You shall eat the fruit of the labor of your hands; you shall be happy, and it shall go well with you. Your wife will be like a fruitful vine within your house; your children will be like olive shoots around your table. Thus shall the man be blessed who fears the Lord."

The Bible consistently teaches us these ways of raising children because ultimately they do not belong to us. They belong to God. Deuteronomy beautifully says, "The Lord is our God, the Lord alone. You shall love the Lord your God with all your heart, and with all your soul, and with all your might. Keep these words that I am commanding you today in your heart. Recite them to your children and talk about them when you are at home and when you are away, when you lie down and when you rise." King Solomon, who received wisdom from God, said, "Train up a child in the way he should go and when he is old he will not depart from it" (Proverbs 22:6). All these commands of God are not just laws, rules, and regulations to be obeyed from the fear of punishment. They are the essence of healthy and happy relationships. Parents will always find the Bible to be the best help in raising children. Through Holy scripture God guides us with His truth for right living. His truth makes possible harmony in our relations with God, with others, with our self, and with nature. Just as our parents were instructed to teach us the ways of righteousness, parents today are accountable to God to instruct their children by word and deed to enjoy God's harmony in all the areas of their lives. Therefore, Ephesians 6: 4, says, "Fathers, do not provoke your children to anger, but bring them up in the discipline and instruction of the Lord." Proverbs 3: 11 – 12, 21 – 23, and 26, instruct children with these words, "My son, do not despise the Lord's discipline or be weary of His reproof, for the Lord reproves him whom He loves, as a father the son in whom he delights... My child, do not let these escape from your sight: keep sound wisdom and prudence, and they will be life for your soul and adornment for your neck. Then you will walk on your way securely and your foot will not stumble... for the Lord will be your confidence and will keep your foot from being caught."

These teachings direct us to the fundamental principles of human life and society. Central in these principles are the Biblical Ten Commandments listed first in Exodus 20: 1 – 17. It is natural for children to put their trust in their parents. In their eyes, parents represent security, authority, truth, justice, and love. God, therefore, entrusts parents with His Commandments so children will develop the essentials of character, discipline, and faith. The Ten Commandments are structured in the following way:

A. The first four identify our Duty to God which are: (1) You shall have no other gods before or in place of the One True God, (2) You shall not make idols and images to worship, or let material things become your god, (3) You shall not misuse the name of God by cursing or by not keeping a promise made to God, (4) You shall remember the Sabbath Day and keep it Holy which means to rest from work and worship the Lord your God one day each week.

B. The fifth commandment is the "Bridge Commandment" representing parents who teach children the ways of God. It says to children that they are (5) To honor their father and mother. This means they are to trust them, respect them, love them, and obey them. It is the only commandment that states a promise. The promise is their days will be many in the land that God gives to them. The parents are in the middle of the Ten Commandments for they nurture children in fulfilling their duty to God, and their duty to others which are identified in the remaining six commandments.

C. These duties to others are: (6) You shall not murder, (7) You shall not be sexually immoral or commit adultery, (8) You shall not steal or take what does not belong to you, (9) You shall not lie or misrepresent the truth, and (10) You shall not covet or be jealous of what others have.

Parents are to teach these commandments to their children in the ways they manage their home with fairness and consistency. Also by being good examples in what they say and do, they are able to provide structure for the development of a child's character and faith. Parents are the fifth commandment which is the bridge which children move across to develop a right relation with God and right relations with others. Children are to honor their parents so as they mature and develop, they can transition their ultimate trust from their father and mother to God. As children grow, they learn that their parents also honor and obey God, and look to Him for their essential needs. Children soon learn that parents are not perfect in every way. Only God is good and perfect. They, therefore, learn from their parents the importance of admitting mistakes and wrongs.

Children benefit greatly when their father and mother apologize, as well as confess selfish ways, and then experience forgiveness. They see that an error or a transgression doesn't destroy family relationships when forgiveness is shared. In homes where there is honesty, humility, and reconciliation, children learn that forgiveness weaves the fabric which holds people together. Parents also learn the restorative power of forgiveness from children. Little children are masters at saying "I'm sorry," forgiving others, and getting on with their lives without holding grudges. I remember many times when our two girls were small children. They would have a falling out with each other, and one would say, "I'm never going to play with you again." Then the other would say, "I'm sorry." In less than five minutes they were playing happily together again without remembering the offense.

Mamie Gene Cole understood children in this way. She wrote for her Church newsletter years ago these thoughts about a child:
"I am the child all the world waits for my coming.
All the earth watches with interest to see what I shall become.
Civilization hangs in the balance,
For what I am, the world of tomorrow will be.
I am the child. I have come into the world, about which I know nothing.
Why I came I know not. How I came I have no clue.
I am curious: I am interested. I am the child.
You hold in your hand my destiny.
You determine, largely, whether I shall succeed or fail.
Give me, I pray you, those things that make for happiness.
Train me, I beg you, that I may be a blessing to the world."

These reflections of a child's first awareness of life are expanded by an unknown author who wrote:

"If a child lives with criticism, he learns to condemn.
If a child lives with hostility, he learns to fight.
If a child lives with fear, he learns to be apprehensive.
If a child lives with pity, he learns
to feel sorry for himself.
If a child lives with jealousy, he learns to feel guilty, but
If a child lives with encouragement, he learns
to be self-confident.
If a child lives with tolerance, he learns to be patient.
If a child lives with praise, he learns to be appreciative.
If a child lives with acceptance, he learns to love.
If a child lives with approval, he learns to like himself.
If a child lives with recognition, he learns to have a goal.
If a child lives with fairness, he learns what justice is.
If a child lives with honesty, he learns what truth is.
If a child lives with sincerity, he learns
confidence in himself and those around him.
If a child lives with Christian faith, he learns
to pray and walk with God every day.
If a child lives with love he learns
that God is love and the world is a wonderful place."

Yes, it is an awesome responsibility to raise children with love, discipline, and self-esteem. The Book of Proverbs is very helpful in giving parents purposeful instruction about teaching children wisdom (2:2), seeking discernment (2:3), understanding the reverence God deserves (2:5), recalling the teaching of fathers and mothers (1:8, 3:1), and obeying God's commandments (4:1-4). But beyond the numerous responsibilities parents have, it is very rewarding to realize the many benefits children bring to their lives. Some of these are:

1. The divine joy of sharing with God in the creation of new life.
2. The sense of increased personal value and importance a child's birth brings to parents.
3. The fun and entertainment they give while watching them grow, play, and learn.
4. The increased humility from a child's innocent love and trust.

5. The lessons of self-giving, discipline, gentleness, and patience parents learn from children.
6. The help and assistance children provide for the household, on the farm, and other work.
7. The pride and recognition children bring parents through activities and accomplishments.
8. The care adult children provide for aging parents.
9. The extending and expanding the influence and witness of the Christian life to others.
10. The improvement of the community, nation, and world by being responsible citizens.

Marriage given of God has the potential of being fruitful and multiplying. Many couples will chose not to have children. Others will yearn to bring children into their home, but unfortunately will learn they are not able to conceive. Husbands and wives who receive the gift of children can be assured that God will bless them greatly if they raise their children for the Glory of the One who makes life possible. After children are born, Jesus says, "Let the little children come to me; do not stop them; for it is to such as these that the kingdom of God belongs. Truly I tell you, whoever does not receive the kingdom of God as a little child will never enter it." And He took the children up in His arms, laid His hands on them, and blessed them (Mark 10: 14-16). One of the first things parents should do after a child is born is to dedicate their son or daughter in a sanctuary of the Lord with thanksgiving.

This presentation of children through the Christian faith of parents and the Church claims God's loving care and protection for them. In the event of their untimely death, Jesus promises eternal life for "unto them belong the Kingdom of God." Parents, confident of Jesus' assurance, are then able to raise their children in Christian homes where they will experience love, peace, joy, truth, forgiveness, and the guidance of right living.

When the children come of age and confess Jesus Christ as their personal Savior, they are baptized in water for the remission of sins. Romans 6: 1-5 visually describes the act of immersion with these words: "All of us who have been baptized into Christ Jesus were baptized into His death. Therefore we have been buried with Him by baptism into death, so that, just as Christ was raised from the dead by the glory of the Father, so we too might walk in newness of life. For if we have been united with Him in a death like His, we will certainly be united with Him in a resurrection like His." In baptism the water is pictured as a grave. Children and others who confess Christ are placed under the water. They are buried just as Jesus was. He died on the cross for the sins of the world. His body was placed in the tomb of Joseph of Arimathea who was one of His disciples (John 19: 38). As believers are raised from the waters of baptism, they symbolically and literally share in the resurrection of Jesus Christ who was raised from the grave on Easter morning.

Parents, therefore, are following the Will of God when they present their children to Jesus Christ for dedication. During their developing years, they begin to prepare their children for Christian baptism — when the children reach the "age of accountability", knowing the difference between right and wrong, they are able to make their personal profession of faith in Jesus Christ. Baptism by immersion in water is a beautiful act of obedience dramatizing the death, burial, and resurrection of Jesus Christ as Romans 6:1-10 clearly describes.

Parents who follow these instructions of our Lord in raising children need to know also that the means of God's Grace is often administered to children through prayer. Each child needs parents who will daily pray, "Gracious Lord, watch over, keep in Your Will, and guide in every way that brings Glory to Your Name, this child You have entrusted to my love and care. Grant that my child will love You and grow in wisdom, and in stature, and in favor with You and others just as Your Son, Jesus, did. Amen." (Luke 2:52).

CHAPTER TWENTY ONE

BE FILLED WITH THE SPIRIT

Ephesians 5: 15-20, *"Be careful then how you live, not as unwise people but as wise, making the most of the time, because the days are evil. So do not be foolish, but understand what the will of the Lord is. Do not get drunk with wine, for that is debauchery; but be filled with the Spirit, as you sing psalms and hymns and spiritual songs among yourselves, singing and making melody to the Lord in your hearts, giving thanks to God the Father at all times and for everything in the name of our Lord Jesus Christ."*

Please read the scripture above carefully and thoughtfully. Meditate upon the meaning of each word. Discover the relevance of these Bible verses to Christian marriage. If you have read through the previous chapters, you probably feel inadequate in doing your part to fulfill God's plan for marriage. God's standard for a man and woman in the Covenant of Marriage is the ideal. We all want what God intends for us to receive and experience. Yet, we are aware that we often fail to deliver the unselfish love, patience, forgiveness, and kindness that God's Ideal Marriage requires.

This is exactly the understanding that a wise person sooner or later realizes. In spite of our best efforts, we can't be the husband or wife who every day is faithful, honest, thoughtful, and giving while cherishing, honoring, protecting, and comforting each other. Without Divine help, we simply cannot do it. We are imperfect people who often sin and fall short of the Glory of God as Romans 3:23 reminds us.

Ephesians 5: 15-20, therefore, is our Good News. It directs us to the Holy Spirit who can and will help us. We can't fulfill the purpose and goals of marriage alone. When we admit our helplessness and call upon God to deliver us from our selfish nature, He gives us His Holy Spirit. Our greatest need in order to achieve true marriage is to be "Filled With The Spirit." I want to say this again. The Holy Spirit is the enabler whose <u>presence</u> within us provides the joy that Ephesians 5 describes! We then can sing as we give thanks to God for His Goodness and mercy.

We can be filled with the Holy Spirit if we are willing to live according to the Will of God. We can't have the Spirit and be like the man in a rural town of Georgia. He preferred being filled with wine more than living God's way. For several consecutive years during the annual Church revival, he would be one of the first to respond to the altar call. He would come down the aisle with outstretched arms and crying out, "Fill me Lord. Fill me with your Holy Spirit." Soon after each revival he would return to his old ways of drinking. The next year when he came forward during the revival asking God to fill him with the Holy Spirit, one lady in the choir shouted, "Don't do it Lord. He leaks."

I guess we all leak. However, each of us can have the Holy Spirit through faith in Jesus Christ as our Savior and obedience to Him as our Lord. God made this possible on the Day of Pentecost according to Acts 2:38. Thousands of people who had gathered in the streets of Jerusalem heard the Good News of God's Love and Salvation in Jesus Christ. They called out to Peter, who had been preaching this Gospel to them: "What shall we do?" Peter answered, "Repent, and be baptized every one of you in the name of Jesus Christ so that your sins may be forgiven; and you will receive the gift of the Holy Spirit." On that day about three thousand persons were baptized, and they received the Holy Spirit.

Jesus, Himself, showed us the way to receive the Holy Spirit. The Gospel of Matthew 3: 13 -17, tells us, "Then Jesus came from Galilee to John at the Jordan, to be baptized by him. John would have prevented Him, saying, 'I need to be baptized by You, and do You come to me?' But Jesus answered him, 'Let it be so now; for it is proper for us in this way to fulfill all righteousness.' Then he consented. And when Jesus had been baptized, just as He came up from the water, suddenly the heavens were opened to Him and He saw the Spirit of God descending like a dove and alighting on Him. And a voice from heaven said, 'This is my Son, the Beloved, with whom I am well pleased.'"

After Jesus fulfilled His earthly ministry and before He ascended to heaven to be one with God, He gave His followers the Great Commission. He said, "All authority in heaven and on earth has been given to Me. Go therefore and make disciples of all nations, baptizing them in the name of the Father and of the Son and of the Holy Spirit, and teaching them to obey everything that I have commanded you. And remember, I am with you always, to the end of the age" (Matthew 28: 18 -20). This is God's plan for everyone to know His Love, be forgiven of sin, redeemed for Abundant and Eternal Life, and filled with the Holy Spirit. When the Holy Spirit abides in us, He makes available three Divine gifts for our journey in this life. They are especially valuable for a Christian marriage.

FIRST, THE HOLY SPIRIT GIVES US TRUTH

Jesus told His disciples, "I am the way, the truth, and the life...The Holy Spirit, whom the Father will send in My name, will teach you everything, and remind you of all that I have said to you" (John 14: 6 & 26). "When the Holy Spirit comes, He will guide you into all the truth...He will glorify Me, because He will take what is Mine and declare it to you" (John 16: 13-14). The presence of the Holy Spirit, therefore, convicts us and the world of deception and sin. The Holy Spirit then leads us to God's Will and Truth. Jesus came into this world "Full of Grace and Truth" (John 1: 14).

The mission of the Holy Spirit is to make known this Truth that sets us free, which establishes honest relationships and communities of unselfish love. A couple came to me years ago needing truth on which to begin their marriage. During our first premarital counseling session, they complimented our Church with their decision to have their wedding ceremony in our beautiful sanctuary. The bride, however, had a special request. She asked that we fulfill her childhood dream of beginning the ceremony with an enactment of the Cinderella Story.

Her plan was for the groom to come onto the chancel with the groomsmen. A chair would be at the end of the center aisle. Each bridesmaid would then enter and be seated in the chair. The groom would try on the bride's "Glass Like Slipper" only to find it didn't fit. After all the bridesmaids were in their places, the bride would make her grand entrance down the center aisle. The groom would help her be seated. He then would try on the beautiful slipper. It would fit perfectly. They would stand and embrace with great joy and delight. The congregation would applaud, and the wedding ceremony would begin.

When she described this drama with such feeling, she could hardly hold back the tears. I was impressed with her plan and respectful of her request. But I gently told her and her fiancé that we could not do this at our Church. She was shocked and disappointed. She asked, "Why not?" I then explained to her that marriage, given and blessed by God, was to begin, mature, and continue on the foundation of truth for as long as you both live. I explained that the fairy tale of Cinderella was a beautiful and fun story. But it wasn't true. I continued by saying, "If your wedding begins in the setting of the Cinderella story, you would be presenting yourself to your groom as the charming maiden anointed by the fairy godmother. Your marriage, therefore, would not begin with truth. It would begin with make believe images of 'living happily together forever after.' However, the reality is that the two of you like all of us are imperfect people who will in spite of your best efforts make mistakes. There will be no fairy godmother that will wave a magic wand to correct all the problems and disappointments you will experience."

I concluded my response by assuring them that the love and blessings of God would be more than enough to sustain them in marriage. He would guide them in all truth through the Holy Spirit. God would enable them to succeed in becoming one as husband and wife based on the reality of who they are, not who they pretend to be. "If this is what you want," I explained, "then I would consider it an honor to officiate at your wedding."

After looking at each other and sighing a few times, they said, "We do want to be honest and start our marriage on truth. We do want God to be pleased with us. We will eliminate the make-believe parts and try to plan our wedding ceremony according to God's Will." I could not have been more pleased. They returned to my study for several more counseling and planning sessions. After their wedding, several months later, they said to me, "We could not be happier."

Truth won out because truth is the first gift of the Holy Spirit. It gives marriage balance and liberates us from illusions, doubts, and fears. Since God is the source of all truth, it is obvious that the closer our relationship is with God, the more we will benefit from His truth. Jesus said, "God is spirit, and those who worship Him must worship in spirit and truth" (John 5:24). As we worship God and meditate upon His Word through the inspiration of scripture, the Holy Spirit guides us in truth. We must not be content to have the Spirit without the Word. It is only through our faithful reading of the Bible that we are able to be filled with the truth of the Holy Spirit. Just as we need daily food to sustain us physically, we need to ask the Holy Spirit to fill us each day with God's truth so we will be spiritually nourished. Husbands and wives need this truth as they seek to make right decisions regarding issues like the following:

1. What should be the priorities and goals of our marriage?
2. In which Church and Bible study groups should we be active?
3. Where can we best advance in our careers and work?
4. How can we schedule our weekly time for each other and our goals?
5. How can we manage our money to honor God, pay bills, and invest in the future?
6. What is God's Will for us regarding credit and borrowing money?
7. What community services can we provide for others, and how often?
8. What recreational and physical fitness activities should we schedule?
9. What is God's Will for us having and raising children?
10. What are the primary moral issues we will live by regarding abortion, gambling, etc.?
11. What will be our civic and political commitments?
12. What family traditions will we honor, and which new ones do we want to start?

We can know the truth for questions like these by being filled with the Holy Spirit. The Holy Spirit will enlighten us with Truth in three ways: (1) through hearing and studying God's inspired Word in the Bible; (2) by praying in the Spirit who "Helps us in our weakness...and intercedes for us" (Romans 8: 26); and (3) seeking righteous counsel from mature Christian men and women. In these ways marriage is established on a solid foundation which strengthens the trust a husband and wife must have in each other.

SECOND, THE HOLY SPIRIT GIVES US POWER

When Christians are filled with the Holy Spirit they have power to be true to their promises, beliefs, and purpose in life and in marriage. Jesus said to His followers, "You will receive power when the Holy Spirit has come upon you; and you will be my witnesses..." (Acts 1:8). This power enables us to live with integrity so others will see in us The Christ who is "The Way, The Truth, and The Life" (John 14: 6). We, therefore, are to be His witnesses in good and bad times. Even in suffering, we have power to be faithful and true. Romans 5: 3-5 confirms this by saying, "Suffering produces endurance, and endurance produces character, and character produces hope, and hope does not disappoint us, because God's love has been poured into our hearts through the Holy Spirit that has been given to us."

A husband and wife can always be confident in each other when the power of the Holy Spirit is present in their lives. They will be able to <u>do</u> what is right according to God's Will and stand against what is wrong according to His Truth. This requires Christian character and courage to follow conscience instead of yielding to the opinion of the crowd or to political correctness. The power of the Holy Spirit makes possible our following the rules, even when others do not, refusing to be prejudiced and hurtful towards anyone, speaking the truth with love even when others disagree, and taking responsibility for our actions without blaming others for our mistakes. Marriage is fortified and sustained with integrity when a couple relies upon the power of the Holy Spirit in their daily lives.

I believe the "Cadet Prayer" reflects this power of the Holy Spirit. It is a prayer that is prayed during chapel services at the United States Military Academy at West Point. The words of this moving prayer are, in part:

O God, our Father! Thou searcher of men's hearts

Help us draw near to Thee in sincerity and truth.

May our religion be filled with gladness and may our worship of Thee be natural.

Strenghten and increase our admiration for honest dealing and clean thinking, and suffer not our hatred or hypocrisy and pretense ever to diminish.

Make us to choose the harder right instead of the easier wrong, and never to be content with a half truth when the whole can be won.

Endow us with courage that is born of loyalty to all that is noble and worthy, that scorns to compromise with vice and injustice and knows no fear when truth and right are in jeopardy.

Grant us new ties of friendship and new opportunities of service. Kindle our hearts in fellowship with those of a cheerful countenance, and soften our hearts with sympathy for those who sorrow and suffer.

THIRD, THE HOLY SPIRIT GIVES US FRUIT FOR DAILY LIVING

God not only wants us to have the Holy Spirit. He commands us in Ephesians 5:18 to: "Be filled with the Spirit." The Holy Spirit gives us <u>truth</u> for right belief and behavior. He also gives us power to accomplish God's Will and Purpose in our lives and marriage. Now in Galatians 5:16 & 22-23, 25, we are instructed to "Live by the Spirit...The fruit of the Spirit is love, joy, peace, patience, kindness, generosity, faithfulness, gentleness, and self-control...If we live by the Spirit, let us also be guided by the Spirit."

In reading this marvelous invitation to "Live by the Spirit," please notice that there is only one fruit of the Holy Spirit. There are nine qualities of the Spirit's fruit, but they represent wholeness for Christian character. We are not given a choice of fruits from which to select as you would at a cafeteria buffet. We need the whole fruit with each of its qualities. Their purpose is to restore harmony in the three primary relationships God intended when He created human life. These are our relationship with God, with others, and with our self.

This is one of the reasons Christianity is so convincingly true. The fruit that God's Spirit provides meets our essential needs! The Apostle Paul discovered this at the time of his conversion from religion and intellectualism to a saving relation with Jesus Christ. He then wrote in Philippians 4: 19, "My God will fully satisfy every need of yours according to His riches in glory in Christ Jesus." The fruit of God's Spirit is not an isolated list of do's and don'ts. Like all the laws and statutes of God, the fruit is for right relationships.

The first three qualities of the Spirit's fruit bring alive our relationship with God. They are:

1. LOVE - "God is love, and those who abide in love abide in God, and God abides in them" (I John 4: 16). When a Jewish lawyer asked Jesus, "Which commandment in the law is the greatest?" Jesus answered, "You shall love the Lord your God with all your heart, and with all your soul, and with all your mind. This is the greatest and first commandment." (Matthew 22:36 – 38). We are able to love God because "He first loved us" (I John 4: 19). Because God gives us the fruit of His Spirit we are able to love God and others with unselfish devotion and caring. I Corinthians 13:13, says it so clearly: "Now faith, hope, and love abide, these three; and the greatest of these is love." We, therefore, should seek this gift of God's Spirit above all others.

2. JOY - When Jesus was born in Bethlehem, an angel of the Lord spoke to the shepherds keeping watch over their flock by night saying, "I am bringing you good news of great joy for all the people: to you is born this day in the city of David a Savior, who is the Messiah, the Lord" (Luke 2: 10 – 11). We have great joy in our relation with God since He has forgiven our sins and restored us as "Children of God" (John 1: 12). This joy is distinct from happiness. Joy is an inner presence of Christ that doesn't come and go with life's changing situations. Happiness however, depends upon the happenings of our circumstances. This is why Jesus says in John 15:5, "I am the vine, you are the branches. Those who abide in me and I in them bear much fruit." True joy is from the Fruit of The Spirit when Christ abides in us.

3. PEACE - Our relationship with God is complete through the Spirit who gives us Peace. Jesus said before His death and resurrection, "Peace I leave with you; My Peace I give to you. I do not give to you as the world gives. Do not let your hearts be troubled, and do not let them be afraid" (John 14: 27). Our hearts are not troubled when our bad choices and wrong behavior are forgiven. Jesus Christ restores us as children of God when we repent and place our faith in Him as Savior and Lord. The Fruit of His Spirit gives us peace and unites us with God. This "peace of God which surpasses all understanding," as Philippians 4:7, describes it, conquers stress, anxiety, fear, and uncertainty of the future. We are able to slow down and cope with the "rapid pace" living of our culture. We then can pray and talk with God as our "Abba, Father," with the assurance He is with us. These three qualities of the Fruit of the Spirit open the way for us to know and worship God with Love, Joy, and Peace.

The next three aspects of the Fruit of the Spirit cultivate harmony and positive relationships with others. They are "Patience, Kindness, and Generosity." They are the social virtues we need as we develop friend-ships, community, and goodwill toward others. They also are the qualities that husbands and wives value and appreciate in each other. Consider the importance of each one of these relational attributes that are given by the Holy Spirit.

4. PATIENCE - This word has its root meaning in the Greek language referring to a person's steadfast calmness when provoked by others. With patience a person acts graciously without unjust criticism towards others even when wrong is done, and disappointments are experienced. Every married couple soon learns the value of this gift. I remember one couple who came for counseling after being married less than one year. Their adjustments to each other's independent ways were most difficult and slow in coming. The wife confessed that they both were very selfish. She said she was more so than her husband. During our discussion of the details of their conflicts, she complimented him by saying, "He is more patient than I am. We probably wouldn't be living together if he hadn't been so patient with me."

I then asked her if she knew how a person becomes more patient. She said she wasn't sure. I opened my Bible to Galatians 5: 22-23, and asked her to read these verses so her husband and I could hear. After reading it, she smiled and said, "So that is where patience comes from. The Fruit of the Holy Spirit <u>gives</u> a Christian patience, kindness, and self-control. I guess I haven't been eating enough fruit lately." We laughed, and all three of us agreed we need to let the Holy Spirit have more control over our moods and emotions.

It is because of patience that the New Testament letter of James 1: 2 – 4, confidently says, "Whenever you face trials of any kind, consider it nothing but joy, because you know that the testing of your faith produces endurance; and let endurance have its full effect, so that you may be mature and complete, lacking in nothing." The Holy Spirit nurtures our maturity and increases our patience so we can respond to others with a positive attitude.

5. KINDNESS – This quality of the Fruit of the Holy Spirit is love acting with goodwill towards others. Before Jesus Christ came into this world there were few institutions of mercy and compassion. This was especially true for the poor and powerless. Jesus always acted with kindness, attracting thousands of people to gather around Him wherever He went. He fed the hungry, healed the sick, forgave the sinner, proclaimed truth to the multitude, and gave believers the Holy Spirit to continue His work. Since His death for humanity and His victorious resurrection, the Holy Spirit has inspired kindness throughout the world. Hospitals, orphanages, mission stations,

Churches, ministries of community development, and schools for all ages have developed. Therefore, a Christian by definition is one who acts with kindness towards others in the name of Jesus Christ.

Kindness is the daily gift husbands and wives can give to each other that brings more joy and satisfaction than material ones could ever provide. It is the fulfillment of the wedding promise to be there for each other in all circumstances of life. One couple I married years ago wrote their vows that simply promised to be kind to each other in sickness and in health, in joy and in sorrow, and in plenty and in want. I asked why this was important to them. The bride said, "I was raised in a home without kindness. I can't live that way any longer. I want our new home to always be a place of kindness no matter what." The Holy Spirit knows we need and want this gift for our happiness. This fruit is provided every day for married couples to share.

6. GENEROSITY – This is the third quality of the trio which the Holy Spirit provides for our relation to and interaction with others. Generosity was a frequent theme in Jesus' teaching. He reversed conventional custom by saying in His Sermon on the Mount, "If anyone strikes you on the right cheek, turn the other also; and if anyone wants to sue you and take your coat, give your cloak as well; and if anyone forces you to go one mile, go also the second mile. Give to everyone who begs from you, and do not refuse anyone who wants to borrow from you." (Mathew 5: 39-42). In other words, Jesus said we are to be generous in all our dealings with others.

    In our selfish nature, we cannot and will not be generous. But through faith in Jesus Christ, who changes our old nature and makes us **new** creatures, we become generous people. The Holy Spirit gives us this gift of generosity that overcomes selfishness. When we allow our Lord to change us in this way, our hearts become like a spring of fresh water that refreshes others in our lives. It reminds me of Spring Lake where I began life guarding at the age of fifteen. It had the largest spring in Fulton County, Georgia. This spring supplied fresh water for the swimming lake that had sandy beaches on three sides. It was amazing how cold and pure the water remained, even on the hottest days of summer. It generously flowed with water during the driest season of the year. One county inspector said, "This is not only the largest spring in the county; it is also the purest water I have ever tested."

A generous heart, like this spring, continually "pours out" goodness in all seasons of life. Marriage as God intends it to be is characterized by the spirit of generosity. A Christian husband and wife, by their very nature in Christ, seek to outdo the other in showing honor and love. They no longer think and act in terms of "me and mine." Instead, their covenant is based on the generosity of the Fruit of the Holy Spirit that counts everything as "ours." They each delight in denying themselves to please the other. An example of this generosity is seen in the story of the wife who said to her husband, "Every time you make sandwiches for us, you always give me the one that has the end pieces of the loaf. Did it ever occur to you that I might not like the end pieces?" His countenance fell as he realized she was not pleased. He said with sadness and disappointment, "The end pieces are my favorite slices of bread. I have always given them to you because I consider them to be the best tasting." She failed to realize his generosity in this small act of unselfish love. Even when our action towards others is misunderstood, generosity is always appreciated.

These three groupings of the qualities of the Holy Spirit's Fruit can be thought of as clusters of grapes. All the fruit is the same, but it is provided for the three areas of our relationships: God, Others, and Self. This third cluster reveals the character and moral reliability of each Christian upon which others can depend. As you consider Faithfulness, Gentleness, and Self-Control, evaluate the importance of each one for a stable and satisfying marriage.

7. FAITHFULNESS – This is the gift of the Holy Spirit that makes our "Yes" to God possible. For example, when Peter confessed Jesus as the Messiah, the Son of the living God, it was the Holy Spirit who revealed the means of his faith statement. Jesus then said to Peter, "Blessed are you, Simon son of Jonah! For flesh and blood has not revealed this to you, but my Father in heaven. And I tell you, you are Peter, and on this rock I will build my Church, and the gates of Hades will not prevail against it" (Matthew 16: 16 – 18). The rock on which the Christian Church is established is the faithfulness of believers in Jesus Christ. The foundation of Christian marriage is the faithfulness of a husband and wife to each other

and to God. The Fruit of the Holy Spirit in both cases enables us to say "Yes" and remain true to our word. Fidelity in little and big things is the evidence of moral character. Jesus indicated this in His "Parable of the Talents." He concludes His story by saying, "You were faithful with a few things, I will put you in charge of many things" (Matthew 25: 21).

The Gospel of John 5: 21 – 24, says that someday everyone will stand before the judgment seat of God where Jesus Christ will judge each of us on the basis of our faithfulness. His judgment will be according to His gift of salvation and our faithfulness. It will not be on the basis of how successful we were in the eyes of the world. Read this scripture for yourself, "Indeed, just as the Father raises the dead and gives them life, so also the Son gives life to whomever He wishes. The Father judges no one but has given all judgment to the Son, so that all may honor the Son just as they honor the Father. Anyone who does not honor the Son does not honor the Father who sent Him. Very truly, I tell you, anyone who hears My Word and believes Him who sent me has eternal life, and does not come under judgment, but has passed from death to life." Romans 5: 1-5, confirms this truth, "Therefore, since we are justified by faith, we have peace with God through our Lord Jesus Christ...because God's love has been poured into our hearts through the Holy Spirit that has been given to us."

This faithfulness given by the Holy Spirit enables us to remain steadfast in our devotion to Christ and to our partner in marriage. The Eleventh Chapter of the Book of Hebrews begins with the declaration, "Now faith is the assurance of things hoped for, the conviction of things not seen." Then it lists the names of men and women who have been faithful. We call this the "Hall of Fame of the Faithful." The Holy Spirit wants our names to be recorded there someday. Also, our names should appear in the "Marriage Hall of Fame" because of our faithfulness to the one we promised our allegiance.

8. GENTLENESS – Jesus had all power and authority in heaven and earth to carry out God's Will during His ministry (Matthew 28: 18). Yet, at the same time, He was the most gentle person who ever lived. Little children were drawn to Him because of His gentleness. All three persons of the Holy Trinity have this attribute. King David in Psalm 18: 35 says about God The Father, "It is the gentleness of

God that has made me great." II Corinthians 10: 1 refers to "the gentleness of Christ" who is God The Son. God The Holy Spirit also has gentleness that is given to all who will live by the Spirit (Galatians 5: 23).

This word "gentleness" never means weakness or timidity. It always means strength that chooses to act toward others with mildness. A good illustration of gentleness is when a wild horse with magnificent strength, speed, and beauty is tamed and harnessed. The horse is now mild and able to use its strength and speed to accomplish the tasks assigned to it. The Fruit of the Holy Spirit gives us this quality to use all our potential and ability to fulfill our purpose in life.

Wives especially like for their husbands to be strong, decisive, and act with purpose. But they want them to be gentle, not overbearing, inconsiderate, and egotistical. Husbands also want their wives to be self-confident and aggressive in pursuit of their life dreams, but with the gift of gentleness. They want them to be nurturing without controlling, criticizing, and neglecting their role as helpmate. Both husband and wife should seek with grateful hearts this Fruit that the Holy Spirit provides for everyday living. It nourishes their marriage and guards against dissatisfaction, separation, and divorce.

9. SELF-CONTROL – The final gift in this cluster of The Holy Spirit's Fruit is greatly needed. It is the power of self-control. We in America live in a culture that thrives on excess. So many people have little restraint toward eating, drinking, smoking, gambling, having sex, pornography, shopping, immoral dressing, over accumulating money and things, talking, getting angry, not forgiving, and procrastinating. Without the Holy Spirit giving us self-control, we will over-indulge in harmful ways.

During the first thirty years of my life, I was naive to the reality of human nature. I was raised in a Christian home, and my friends and neighbors were honest and decent people. Our small Georgia town was safe and friendly. We believed right was right and wrong was wrong. I knew there was evil in the world, but I assumed that only a small percentage of humanity was immoral and dishonest according to God's standard of righteousness. However, as I matured in the Christian Ministry and became more involved in the personal lives of many people, I discovered that my assumptions were flawed. Every one of us is by nature sinful and selfish. We live in a fallen world. We all are inclined to know what is right and good, but a power beyond our control often tempts us to do the opposite. The Apostle Paul described our plight in Romans 7: 15-19, "I do not do what I want, but I do the very thing I hate. Now if I do what I do not want, I agree that the law is good. But in fact it is no longer I that do it, but sin that dwells within me. For I know that nothing good dwells within me, that is, in my flesh. I can will what is right, but I cannot do it. For I do not do the good I want, but the evil I do not want is what I do."

Jesus dealt with this fact of human nature in the Garden of Gethsemane on the night He was betrayed. He had asked Peter and His disciples to watch and pray with Him as He sought God's Will. They fell asleep when He needed their support and prayers. He said to Peter, "The Spirit indeed is willing, but the flesh is weak."

Paul declares the answer to our human dilemma when he says, "Wretched man that I am! Who will rescue me from this body of death? Thanks be to God through Jesus Christ our Lord" (Romans 7: 24-25)! Jesus Christ delivers us, forgives us, and gives us the Fruit of The Holy Spirit. It is our transformed lives and the power of the Holy Spirit that enable us to live in this corrupt world, but not be of it any longer.

This self-control is what we must have to live effectively for God and others. Without this Fruit of The Holy Spirit, we will fall victim to immorality, corruption, and unfaithfulness like so many movie and TV stars, politicians, religious leaders, athletes, business executives, and average citizens like you and me. With The Holy Spirit filling us and nourishing us with His Fruit, we can have self-control. We can be strong in the Lord <u>and</u> faithful to our purpose in life. We can control our time, our habits, and our commitments. We can be successful in marriage and true to our promises to love, honor, and cherish each other as long as we live.

There is therefore, nothing more urgent and important for a husband and wife to do than to be filled with the Holy Spirit and devoted to these three **ways of life** presented in this chapter:

1. LIVE IN THE TRUTH OF THE HOLY SPIRIT
2. LIVE BY THE POWER OF THE HOLY SPIRIT
3. LIVE WITH THE FRUIT OF THE HOLY SPIRIT

LOVE'S FULFILLMENT

Love is within every one of us. I believe it seeks fulfillment through commitment just as a magnet searches for metal with which to bond. When the passion of love between a man and woman reaches the level of decision to share life together, there will "Always Be A Wedding." We find this to be true in all circumstances, places, and times of human living.

A moving illustration of this natural attraction is the true story of Lilly Lax and Ludwig Friedman. Lilly was raised in Zarica, Czechoslovakia and met Ludwig during World War II. Lilly's parents and two brothers were marked for extermination at Auschwitz death camp. She and her two sisters, Ilona and Eva, somehow survived the long journey of persecution, hunger, disease, and grief during the war years. Most of the members of Ludwig's family were also killed by Hitler's regime.

In spite of the unspeakable horrors they endured, Lilly's and Ludwig's love would not be denied. They promised their faithfulness to each other and planned a wedding early in the new year of 1946. The one request Lilly made to Ludwig was for him to help her find a white gown in which to be married. He was only twenty one at the time and living in the Bergen Belsen Displaced Person's Camp. He worked part time distributing food to the hungry and destitute people who survived the war. He wanted to fulfill Lilly's dream for their wedding, but in his poverty all he could do was pray for God's help.

One day while Ludwig was working, a former German pilot walked into the food distribution center. He wanted to trade a worthless parachute for several packs of cigarettes and two pounds of coffee beans. When Ludwig saw the white silk parachute, his heart began to race with anticipation. He quickly made the trade, believing God had answered his prayer for Lilly's wedding dress. His supervisor told him he could have the parachute since it had no value to the center.

Lilly's tears of joy flowed down her cheeks when she opened her eyes to receive Ludwig's surprise. She couldn't believe her good fortune. She rushed to her friend, Miriam, who was a seamstress, and asked if she could make her a wedding gown. Miriam welcomed the challenge. In two weeks of work, she fashioned the six parachute panels into an elegant long sleeved gown with a rolled collar and a fitted waist that tied in the back with a stylish bow. She then sewed the leftover material into a matching white shirt for the groom.

On January 27, 1946, more than four hundred people came out on a snowy day in the town of Celle to attend Lilly's and Ludwig's wedding. Love was again the victor over the forces of darkness and despair. They proved that even in the worst of times there can be "Always A Wedding."

Six months later, Lilly's sister, Ilona, wore this wedding gown when she married Max Traeger. After her sister's wedding, seventeen other brides, according to Lilly's count, joyfully used this unique gown on their wedding day. About a year later, Lilly and Ludwig received another great blessing. They were awarded visas to the United States when President Harry Truman granted permission for 100,000 people who were living in the Displaced Person's Camps to immigrate to America.

What became of Lilly's wedding gown? She of course brought it with her when she came to America. Then when the U.S. Holocaust Memorial Museum in Washington, D.C. was opened in 1993, a special showcase was designed to house this historic dress. It is there on display as a shining symbol of marriage that gives fulfillment to the love of a man and woman.

I pray that this book will also be a symbol of truth and a useful guide for couples whose love is in the process of BEGINNING a marriage, RENEWING a marriage, or RESCUING a marriage.

Christian Wedding Ceremony

ENTRANCE

As people gather, music appropriate to the praise of God may be offered.

At the appointed time, the groom and other members of the wedding party take their assigned places and stand before the officiating minister.

If the Unity Candle is to be a part of the ceremony, the mothers, as they are escorted in, usually light the two candles beside the larger center candle.

The congregation stands as the bride enters, and remains standing through the Invocation.

SENTENCES OF SCRIPTURE

The minister quotes the following verses of scripture:

"God is love, and those who abide in love abide in God, and God abides in them." 1 John 4:16

"For God so loved the world that He gave His only Son, that whoever believes in Him should not perish but have eternal life." John 3:16

THE INVOCATION

The minister then prays: "Gracious God, how excellent is your name in all the earth! You are divine love. You have created us in love and for love. It is Your love and our love that brings us together on this special day. Grant us, therefore, O God, the joy of Your Presence as we ask for Your blessing upon

_____ and _____

who seek the covenant of marriage.

Provide them, O God, with the gifts of Your Holy Spirit so that with steadfast love they will honor the promises they make in this sacred hour, through Jesus Christ Our Lord and Savior. Amen."

(The congregation may be seated)

THE AFFIRMATION OF MARRIAGE

The minister then says to the congregation:

"Dearly beloved, we are gathered here in the presence of God as families and friends to witness the joining of this man and this woman in Holy Matrimony. Marriage is a sacred union, instituted of God in the time of creation, and adorned by our Lord Jesus Christ by his presence at a wedding ceremony and feast in Cana of Galilee where He performed His first miracle by turning the water into wine.

Marriage is also commended by Holy Scripture to be honorable among all people; and therefore, is not by any to be entered into lightly and unadvisedly, but reverently, soberly, discreetly and in devotion to God. Into this happy estate _____ and _____ come now to be joined. As their families and friends, we extend to them our love, encouragement, and prayerful support as they begin their marriage as husband and wife."

THE DECLARATIONS OF INTENT

The minister asks the groom:

"_____, will you have _____

as your wife, to live together according to God's own ordinance in the covenant of marriage? Will you love her, honor her, cherish and protect her in sickness and in health, and forsaking all others keep yourself only unto her so long as you both shall live?"

The groom answers:

   "I will."

The minister asks the bride:

"_____, will you have _____

as your husband, to live together according to God's own ordinance in the covenant of marriage? Will you love him, honor him, cherish and comfort him in sickness and in health, and forsaking all others keep yourself only unto him so long as you both shall live?"

The bride answers:

   "I will."

THE PRESENTATION OF THE BRIDE

The minister asks the father or designated escort:

"Who presents this woman to be married to this man?"

The father or escort responds by saying:

   "I do" or "Her mother and I are happy to present _____
   in marriage to _____."

If she has a veil over her face, he may lift it at this time. He places her right hand in the groom's right hand, and kisses her on her cheek. He then moves back, being careful not to step on the train of the gown, and sits besides the bride's mother unless it is more appropriate to sit elsewhere.

THE GIFT OF MARRIAGE AND PERSONAL STATEMENTS

The minister will reflect on the nature of marriage as God's gift based upon the following beliefs:

"God provides to the faithful many spiritual gifts that sustain marriage, which include love, joy, peace, patience, kindness, and forgiveness."

Scriptures such as Genesis 2, I Corinthians 13, Colossians 3: 12-17, Matthew 7:24-27 or Ephesians 5:21-32 *may be used along with other sacred poetry and thoughts that are meaningful to the couple.*

God created us male and female,

And gave us marriage

So that husband and wife may help and comfort each other,

Living faithfully together in plenty and want,

In joy and sorrow,

In sickness and in health,

Throughout all their days.

God gave us marriage to reveal the very essence of His own Image, and

For the full expression of love between a man and a woman.

In marriage a woman and a man belong to each other,

And with affection and tenderness

Freely give themselves to each other.

God gave us marriage

For the well-being of human society,

For the ordering of family life,

And for the birth and nurturing of children.

God gave us marriage as a holy mystery

In which a man and a woman are joined together,

And become one flesh,

Just as Christ is one with the Church.

In marriage, husband and wife are called to a new way of life,

Being subject each to the other,

Created, ordered, and blessed by God.

This way of life must not be entered into carelessly,

Or from selfish motives,

But responsibly and prayerfully.

We rejoice that marriage is given by God.

Blessed by our Lord Jesus Christ,

And sustained by the Holy Spirit.

Therefore, let marriage be held in honor among all."

The minister then says to the couple:

"If it is your resolve to receive this Gift of God and enter into the true covenant of Marriage, let us go to the Altar of God where you will make your vows and promises."

The minister steps up to the Chancel and takes the central place in front of the Altar. The couple then steps up, followed by the best man, maid of honor, flower girl, and the ring bearer. The bride gives her bouquet to the maid of honor. The couple then faces each other and joins hands. The minister leads the groom and the bride in declaring their vows.

THE EXCHANGE OF VOWS

Repeating after the minister, the groom says to the bride:

"I, _____ take you, _____

to be my wife. I promise before God and these witnesses to be your faithful and loving husband; in plenty and in want; in joy and in sorrow; in sickness and in health; as long as we both shall live; according to God's Holy Ordinance."

Repeating after the minister, the bride says to the groom:

"I, _____ take you, _____

to be my husband. I promise before God and these witnesses, to be your faithful and loving wife; in plenty and in want; in joy and in sorrow; in sickness and in health; as long as we both shall live; according to God's Holy Ordinance."

THE GIVING OF RINGS

When the rings are presented, the minister will ask the couple to wear them as gifts of their abiding love, as signs of their covenant with God, who is the Alpha and the Omega, the beginning and the end (Revelation 21:6), and as symbols of their faithfulness which the purity of precious metals represents.

The minister may say the following prayer:

"By your blessing, O God, may these rings be to

_____ and _____

symbols of unending love and faithfulness, reminding them of the covenant they have made this day, through Jesus Christ our Lord and Savior. Amen."

Repeating after the minister, the groom says:

"_____, I give you this ring with all my love, as a sign of our covenant, in the name of the Father, and of the Son, and of the Holy Spirit. Amen."

Repeating after the minister, the bride says:

"_____, I give you this ring with all my love, as a sign of our covenant, in the name of the Father, and of the Son, and of the Holy Spirit. Amen."

THE UNITY CANDLE

The minister invites the couple to light the Unity Candle.

The minister may explain that the Unity Candle represents the new home established by this marriage and the two side candles represent the families and homes from which the Groom and Bride come. The side candles usually are lighted by the mothers at the beginning of the ceremony, indicating the love and blessings bestowed upon this marriage. All three candles remain lighted.

The minister then quotes the words of Jesus Christ in Mark 10: 6-8:

"But from the beginning of creation, 'God made them male and female'. For this reason a man and woman shall leave father and mother, cleave to each other, and the two shall become one flesh."

THE CELEBRATION OF HOLY COMMUNION

The couple then returns to the front of the kneeling bench and kneels. Holy Communion may be served, usually just to the couple, to celebrate the New Covenant in the life of Jesus Christ, and the covenant of marriage that God gives. However, it may be offered to everyone attending the wedding.

The couple is encouraged to bring their own chalice for communion from which they will drink for the first time on their wedding day. It will become a treasured item to symbolize God's active presence in their lives and home. Hopefully they will drink from it every year on their wedding anniversary, and at other special times, to renew their promises and celebrate God's sustaining Grace. As the rings represent the promises of the husband and wife, so the chalice represents God's promise to sustain marriage with divine resources of love, joy, peace, grace and forgiveness through the faith of the couple. Receiving communion in the wedding ceremony is a witness that the couple will not rely just on themselves for the success of their marriage. They are promising to look to God every day for love, hope, patience, wisdom, guidance and help in their living together.

THE PRAYER OF BLESSING

The minister joins hands on the kneeling bench with the couple and prays:

"God of love and giver of all Grace, bestow your blessing upon
_____and_____
whom You have united in Holy Marriage. As we join hands now with You, make them truly one in their love and purpose. Grant that their wills may be so knit together in Your Will, and their spirits in Your Spirit, that they may grow in love, peace and joy with You and each other all the days of their lives.
May _____ now remember to pray for his wife, _____ each day, knowing that there is no more affectionate and considerate thing he can ever do for her than lift her up to Your throne of Grace in prayer, asking that you always keep her safe wherever she is, and in good health, forever happy in his love.
May _____now remember to pray for her husband, _____ each day that he receives the fullness of Your blessing in all things and be forever happy in her love.
Grant that all who have witnessed these vows today will find their lives strengthened, and that all who are married depart with their own promises renewed, through Jesus Christ our Lord. Amen."
The couple stands, faces each other, and holds hands.

THE ANNOUNCEMENT OF MARRIAGE

The minister then joyfully says:

"For as much as _____ and
_____ have promised to be faithful
and true to each other, and have made their solemn vows before God
and all of us assembled here as their witnesses by giving and receiving
rings and by joining hands, now therefore, in accordance with the laws
and grace of God, who alone gives marriage, as an ordained minister of
the Gospel of Jesus Christ, I happily pronounce them husband and wife.
Those whom God has joined together let no one ever separate!"

THE BENEDICTION

*The minister asks for God's blessing upon the couple and the congregation
with these words of benediction:*

"May the grace of Christ attend you,

The love of God surround you,

The Holy Spirit keep you,

That you may live in faith,

Abound in hope,

And grow in love,

Both now and forevermore. Amen."

The couple may kiss.

THE PRESENTATION OF THE COUPLE

The Minster says:

"It is now my privilege to present to you:

Mr. and Mrs. _____."

THE RECESSIONAL

The newly-married couple and the wedding party exit.

A CHRISTIAN AFFIRMATION OF FAITH

As members of the Christian Church, we confess that Jesus is the Christ,
the Son of the Living God, and proclaim Him Lord and Savior
of the world.
In Christ's name and by his Grace we accept
our mission of witness and service to all people.
We rejoice in God, Maker of heaven and earth, and in the
covenant of love which
binds us to God and one another.
Through baptism into Christ we enter into newness of life and
are made one with the whole people of God.
In the communion of the Holy Spirit, we are joined together in
discipleship and in obedience to Christ.
At the table of the Lord, we celebrate with thanksgiving the
saving acts and presence of Christ.
Within the whole Church, we receive the gift of ministry and
the light of Scripture.
In the bonds of Christian faith we yield ourselves to God that
we may serve the One whose kingdom has no end.
Blessing, glory and honor be to God forever. Amen.

BIBLIOGRAPHY

Achtemeier, Elizabeth (1976). *The Committed Marriage.* Philadelphia, PA: The Westminster Press.

Briscoe, Stuart & Jill (1994). *Marriage Matters! Growing Through the Differences and Surprises of Life Together.* Wheaton, IL: Harold Shaw Publishers.

Burkett, Larry (1999). *Crisis Control in the New Millennium: Seven Key Principles for Your Financial Prosperity.* Nashville, TN: Thomas Nelson Publishers Inc.

Cymbala, Jim (1999). *Fresh Faith: What Happens When Real Faith Ignites God's People.* Grand Rapids, MI: Zondervan Publishing.

Everett, Wm. J. (1985). *Blessed be the Bond: Christian Perspectives on Marriage and Family.* Philadelphia, PA: Fortress Press.

Gray, John (1992). *Men Are from Mars, Women Are from Venus: A Practical Guide for Improving Communication and Getting What You Want in Your Relationships.* N.Y., N.Y.: HarperCollins Publishers Inc.

Hart, Archibald and Morris, Sharon (2003). *Safe Haven Marriage: Building a Relationship You Want to Come Home.* Nashville, TN: W Publishing Group, a division of Thomas Nelson, Inc.

Hartley, Willard & Chalmers, Jennifer Hartley (1998). *Surviving An Affair.* Grand Rapids, MI: Baker Book House.

Hemfelt, Robt & Susan; Minirth, Frank & Mary Alice; Newman, Brian & Deborah (1991). *Passages of Marriage: Five Growth Stages that will Take Your Marriage to Greater Intimacy and Fulfillment.* Nashville, TN: Thomas Nelson

Ingram, Chip (2003). *Love, Sex, and Lasting Relationships: God's Prescription for Enhancing Your Love Life.* Grand Rapids, MI: Baker Books.

Hendrix, Harville (1988). *Getting The Love You Want: A Guide for Couples.* N.Y., N.Y.: Harper & Row Publishers Inc.

Lucado, Max (2006) *Facing Your Giants: A David and Goliath Story for Everyday People.* Nashville, TN: W Publishing Group.

Nowell, Glenn (2001). *Unconditional Joy: How to Get It, Have It, and Keep It.* New Kensington, PA: Whitaker House.

Parrott, Les and Parrott, Leslie (1995). *Saving Your Marriage Before It Starts: Seven Questions to Ask Before (and After) You Marry.* Grand Rapids, MI: Zondervan Publishing House

Rainey, Dennis (1993). *Building Your Marriage: Personal Study Guide.* Little Rock, AR: Family Life Publishing.

Rainey, Dennis, editor, w/Boehi, D., Nelson, B., Schulte, J. & Shadrach, L. (1997). *Preparing for Marriage: The Complete Guide to Help You Discover God's Plan for a Lifetime of Love.* Ventura, CA.: Gospel Light

Sager, Clifford. (1976). *Marriage Contracts and Couple Therapy: Hidden Forces in Intimate Relationships.* N.Y., N.Y.: Brunner/Mazel

Smedes, Lewis (1984). *Forgive and Forget: Healing the Hurts We Don't Deserve.* N.Y., N.Y.: Harper & Row Publishers Inc.

Sweazey, George E. (1966). *In Holy Marriage: A Guide to Making Marriage Work.* N.Y., N.Y.: Harper & Row Publishers.

Swindoll, Charles (2006). *Marriage: From Surviving to Thriving Workbook.* Nashville, TN: W Publishing Group, a division of Thomas Nelson, Inc.

Wangerin, Walter (1990). *As For Me and My House: Crafting Your Marriage to Last.* Nashville, TN: W Publishing Group, a division of Thomas Nelson, Inc.

Wheat, Ed (1988). *The First Years of Forever: For Engaged and Newly Married Couples.* Grand Rapids, MI: Zondervan Publishing House.

Wilke, Richard (1973). *Tell Me Again, I'm Listening.* Nashville, TN.: Abingdon Press.

Yagel, Bobbie & Myron (1995). *Fifteen Minutes to Build a Stronger Marriage: Weekly Togetherness for Busy Couples.* Wheaton, IL: Tyndale House Publishers.

Dr. Collins will gladly do his best to provide you with prayerful support, encouragement, and pastoral guidance for Beginning, Renewing, and Rescuing your marriage.

You may contact Dr. Jim Collins at AlwaysaWedding@aol.com or P.O. Box 385, Young Harris, GA 30582

LaVergne, TN USA
16 February 2011
216674LV00004B/87/P